M + G. MURTON.

THE CITY
LONDON'S SQUARE MILE

ALAN JENKINS

VIKING KESTREL

AUTHOR'S ACKNOWLEDGMENTS

The author wishes to thank members and officers of the Corporation of London, the staff of the Corporation of London Public Relations Office, and the Press Office of the Barbican Centre for information and assistance.

VIKING KESTREL

Published by the Penguin Group
27 Wrights Lane, London W8 5TZ, England
Viking Penguin Inc., 40 West 23rd Street, New York, New York 10010, USA
Penguin Books Australia Ltd, Ringwood, Victoria, Australia
Penguin Books Canada Ltd, 2801 John Street, Markham, Ontario, Canada L3R 1B4
Penguin Books (NZ) Ltd, 182–190 Wairau Road, Auckland 10, New Zealand

Penguin Books Ltd, Registered Offices: Harmondsworth, Middlesex, England

First published 1988

Copyright © Alan Jenkins, 1988

All rights reserved.
Without limiting the rights under copyright
reserved above, no part of this publication may be
reproduced, stored in or introduced into a retrieval system,
or transmitted, in any form or by any means (electronic, mechanical,
photocopying, recording or otherwise), without the prior
written permission of both the copyright owner and
the above publisher of this book

This book was designed and produced by
The Rainbird Publishing Group Ltd,
27 Wrights Lane, London W8 5TZ

Filmset in Caledonia

Printed in Italy

Designer: Lester Cheeseman
Production: Sara Hunt
Indexer: Jane Parker

British Library Cataloguing in Publication Data
Jenkins, Alan
The City: London's Square Mile
1. London (England)
I. Title
942.1'2085'8   DA677

ISBN 0–670–81948–4

ILLUSTRATION ACKNOWLEDGMENTS

(Numbers in italics refer to pages on which black and white illustrations occur)

Corporation of London (Public Relations Office): 8, 13, 16 (photo: Clive Totman), 17 (above and below), 18 (above), 23 (photo: David Steen), 24, 28, 34, 48 (photo: George Tanner), 50–1 (photo: Peter Bloomfield), 56, 57, 58, 66; (Records Office): 7 *(below)*, 59; Mary Evans Picture Library: 68–9, 77 *(below)*; Fotomas Index, London: 45; Tim Graham Picture Library: 80; Guildhall Library: 9, 15, 19, 22 *(above)*, 31, 38, 40, 44, 54, 78–9; Guildhall School of Music and Drama: 55 (photo: Edward Roberts); Angelo Hornak: 12, 14, 21, 25, 26–7, 29, 30, 32–3 (below), 35, 37, 39, 41, 42, 43, 46, 47, 49, 52, 60, 70 (all), 81, 82 (both), 83 (all), 85, 86, 87, 89, 90; Lloyd's of London: 32; The London International Financial Futures Exchange: title page; Museum of London: 6, 7 *(above)*, 11, 18 (below), 22 *(below)*, 36, 61, 62, 63, 64, 65, 84; Fritz von der Schulenburg: 53; Brian Shuel: 17 (centre), 72, 73, 74, 75, 76, 77 (above); Society of Antiquaries of London: 10.

Previous page: *Traders on the floor of the London International Financial Futures Exchange.*

CONTENTS

ROMAN LONDON	6
'LIBERTIES AND FREE CUSTOMS'	8
GUILDHALL	12
THE MAYORALTY	16
ADMINISTERING THE SQUARE MILE	23
THE FINANCIAL CITY	31
FOUR BRIDGES	35
THE CITY'S HEALTH	40
MARKETS: WHOLESALE AND RETAIL	42
LAW AND ORDER	45
THE BARBICAN CENTRE	48
THE CITY'S SCHOOLS	54
CITY LIBRARIES	58
THE MUSEUM OF LONDON	61
FROM WOODS AND COMMONS TO CITY GARDENS	67
CUSTOMS AND TRADITIONS	71
EXPLORING THE CITY'S CHURCHES	78
TAKING TIME OUT	89
INDEX	91

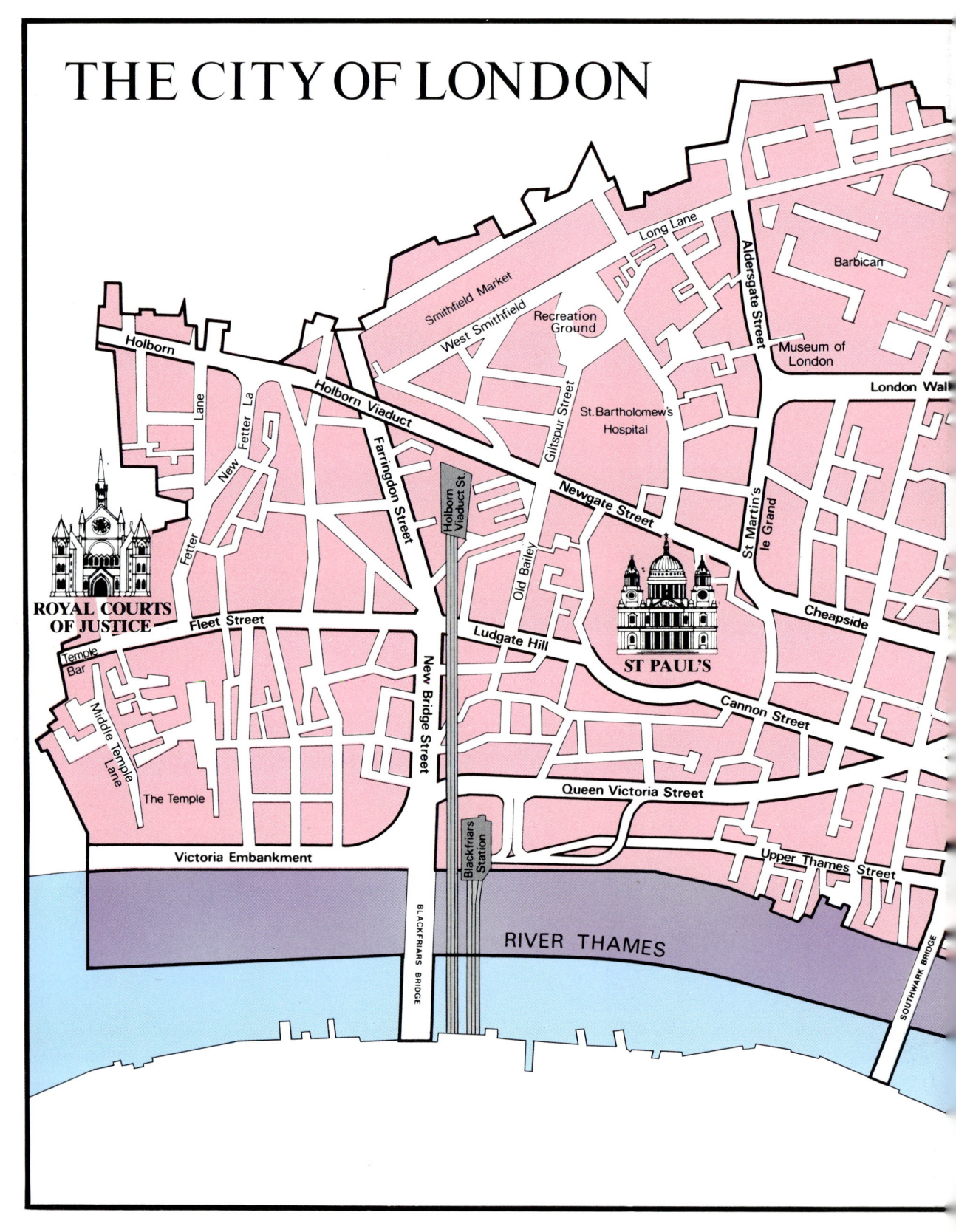

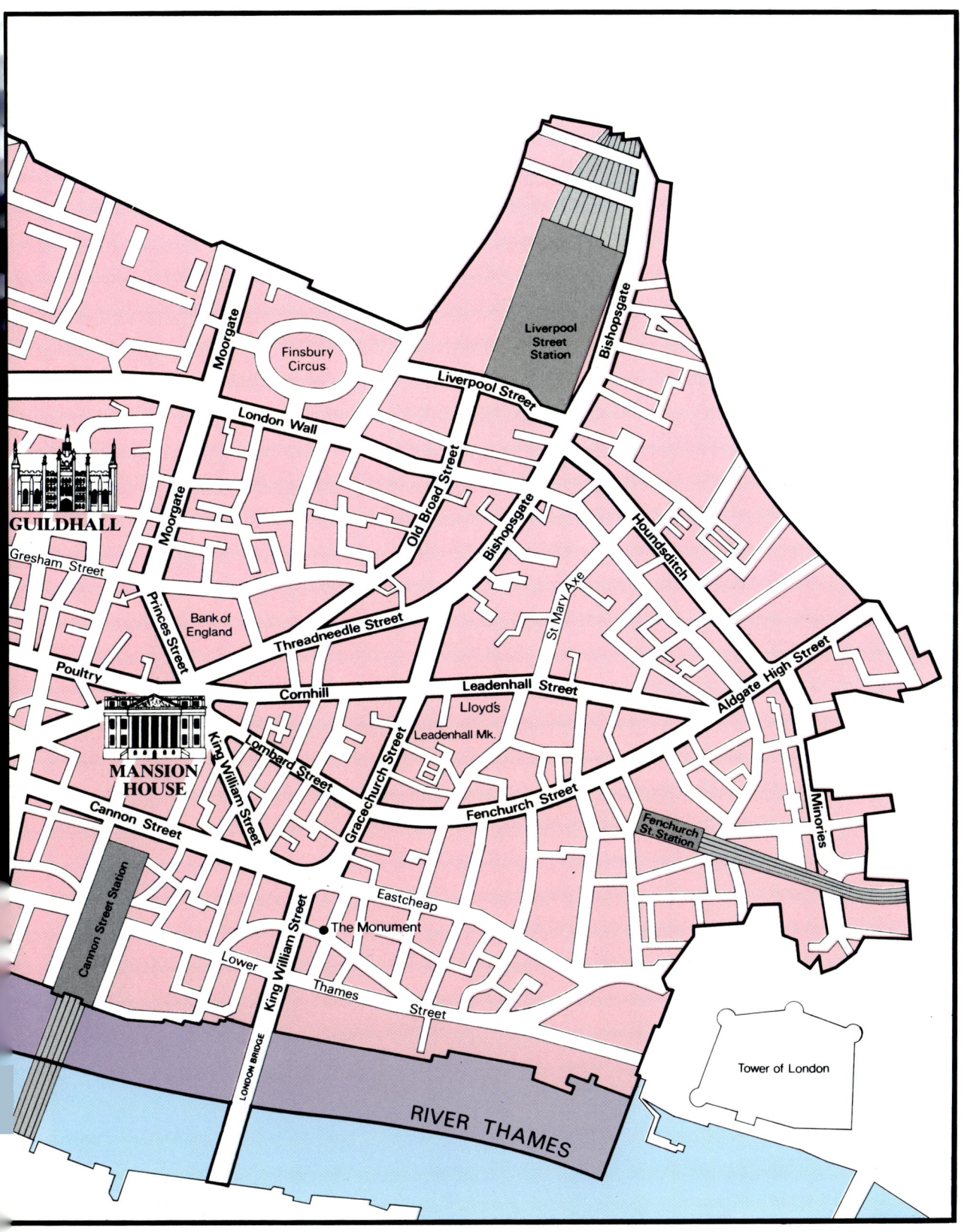

ROMAN LONDON

There is no real evidence to suggest that there was a pre-Roman settlement in London. Certainly Julius Caesar, who invaded Britain briefly in 55 and 54 BC makes no mention of it, and it is now generally accepted that London was founded in about AD 50 by Aulus Plautius and his successors as a port and international trading centre.

The site on which the Romans built the city they called Londinium was probably the lowest point above the estuary of the Thames at which the river could be forded as well as the highest point at which the tidal water could accommodate ships. In 1981 archaeologists located part of what is thought to have been the first, wooden, bridge across the Thames, just south of Wren's Monument, near the present London Bridge.

The city flourished, and the Roman historian Tacitus, writing in the early 2nd century, described it as having been 'a busy emporium' in the 1st century which 'did not rank as a Roman settlement but was an important centre for businessmen and merchandise'. This city was razed to the ground in AD 61 by the rebellious Queen Boudicca, but by then it was sufficiently well established to be rebuilt. A fortress was later constructed in the early 2nd century in the present Cripplegate area and by c.200 a defensive wall encircling the city had been completed. This wall, parts of which still remain, determined London's shape for more than a thousand years.

Roman London probably reached the height of its prosperity in the mid-2nd century. It had become the administrative capital of the

Reconstruction of Londinium's busy waterfront c.AD 100. Pudding Lane lies to the right of the wooden road bridge, with stone-built warehouses opening on to the timber quays.

Marble head of Mithras found in 1954 at the site of the 3rd-century temple in Walbrook devoted to the god's worship.

province Britannia, as well as its financial and commercial centre. The remains of a basilica, public baths and other buildings including a later temple to the god Mithras are all evidence of a flourishing and wealthy colony. By the end of the 3rd century, however, the Roman empire was already in decline, and London declined with it.

At the beginning of the 5th century the barbarian threat to the empire was increasing, and Roman troops were finally withdrawn from Britain to defend Rome itself. For the next 500 years London's history is unclear. It is not even known whether the Saxon invaders who followed the Romans occupied the city, although it was important enough in 604 to warrant the appointment of a bishop, Mellitus. The first church dedicated to St Paul was built at this time but the city's conversion to Christianity was short-lived.

The Danes were a constant menace to London from the 9th century onwards. They attacked the city in 851 but were driven out in 886 by Alfred, the Wessex king who united the Saxon kingdoms of England for the first time. He re-fortified the walls, and encouraged the city's restoration. London (called Lundunberg) prospered despite continual incursions by the Danes after 980. The Danish king Canute and his son ruled England for more than two decades until the throne was restored to Edward the Confessor in 1042. Edward was responsible for building a palace and abbey at Westminster, establishing a second centre for London which was in due course to become the city's political hub. The original City (which we will now refer to as 'the City', to distinguish it from the rest of London) maintained its pre-eminence as a commercial centre, but it was still London's political centre when William the Conqueror came to claim the English throne following the death of his second cousin, the Confessor, in 1066.

William granted the City a charter, which still exists and is kept in the strong room of the Records Office at Guildhall. Addressed to William, the Bishop, and Geoffrey, the Portreeve, it gave greetings to 'all the citizens in London, French and English, in friendly fashion', and promised to preserve the rights and privileges they had enjoyed under Edward the Confessor.

The relationship between the City and successive monarchs was to be one of wariness and mutual suspicion for many centuries as the City became increasingly powerful and jealous of its rights, and the monarchy equally anxious to assert its authority. Having granted the City its charter, William expressed his mistrust by building 'strongholds... in the town against the fickleness of the vast and fierce population'. These included the White Tower, built on the Roman walls, and now part of the Tower of London.

The charter granted to the citizens of London by William I in 1067.

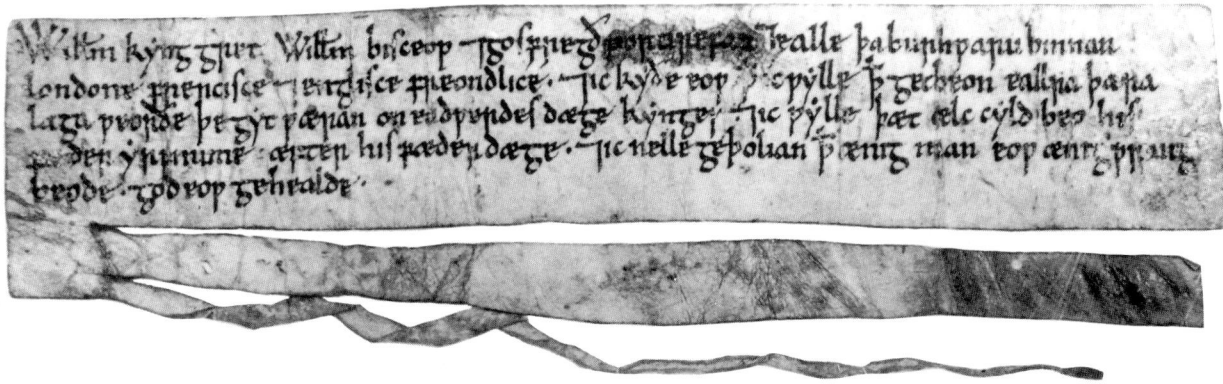

'LIBERTIES AND FREE CUSTOMS'

Within the old Roman walls, the City of London continued to grow and prosper commercially under the Normans and Plantagenets. Although very few buildings survived the Great Fire of 1666, the City's medieval past is preserved today in many of its streets, named after the traders and merchants who lived and worked there. Wood Street, Milk Street, Bread Street, and Poultry are all streets off Cheapside called after the provisions sold there. Lombard Street was a banking precinct named after Lombard merchants, and the name Mincing Lane refers to the 'mynchens' or nuns of a nearby convent.

Medieval trades and crafts were centred around guilds or trade associations. These probably had their origins in the religious associations of Saxon times whose members usually followed the same occupation. The guilds continued to be concerned with the spiritual welfare of their members but increasingly they took on the role of trade regulation and protection. They trained apprentices and ensured that high standards of skill and quality of workmanship were maintained within their respective crafts. Gradually they acquired various rights and privileges, including control over wages, prices, and competition. In due course these were embodied in royal charters, often given in return for financial support of the monarch. The first was granted to the weavers *c.*1155 by Henry I.

The growing influence and prosperity of the guilds was further recognized by granting many of them livery status. This gave senior members the right to wear a distinctive livery or costume, still worn today by the officers of livery companies on ceremonial occasions. There was intense rivalry between the livery companies, which sometimes led to skirmishes in the streets. An order of precedence was finally laid down by the Lord Mayor and Aldermen in 1515 and still exists today. The first five are the Mercers, Grocers, Drapers, Fishmongers, and Goldsmiths. The Skinners and Merchant Taylors were given an equal placing, and took it in turn to be sixth and seventh each year: this is popularly said to be the origin of the phrase 'at sixes and sevens'. The remaining places were taken by the Haberdashers, Salters, Ironmongers, Vintners and Clothworkers.

The livery companies were (and are to this day) generous with their wealth and quick to initiate and support good causes. In particular they have founded some excellent schools. The Mercers administer St Paul's School, founded by Dean Colet, and St Paul's Girls' School, among others. The Grocers founded three schools at Oundle, including the public school.

The guilds and livery companies had always been closely involved in the government of the City, and by the 14th century the mayor was nearly always elected from amongst their members. The first mayor was Henry Fitz-Ailwyn, who took office *c.*1189 and held it for many years until his death. Before this the portreeve had been the first officer of the City, 'port' being an Old English word for a market town. On 9 May 1215 the City was granted a new charter by King John. This gave its citizens the important right to elect their own mayor, on an

A reception room in Fishmongers' Hall, one of many magnificent livery halls in the City.

King George V and Queen Mary at Temple Bar in 1935, on their way to St Paul's Cathedral to attend a service of thanksgiving for the King's Silver Jubilee. The Lord Mayor is offering the reversed Pearl Sword to the monarch.

annual basis. A few weeks later Magna Carta was sealed at Runnymede. It confirmed this and other rights in these words:

> And the City of London shall have all its ancient liberties and free customs, both by land and water. And furthermore we wish and grant that all other cities, boroughs, towns and ports shall have all their liberties and free customs.

The rights granted to the City by King John were of great significance as his charter was the foundation of the City's independent self-government in municipal matters. The relationship between mayor and monarch is symbolized in a ceremony which dates back to medieval times and still takes place when the monarch visits the City in state. The sovereign is met at the site of the old Temple Bar (now demolished but once a gateway marking the City's western limits). The Lord Mayor stands with the Pearl Sword (said to have been a gift to the City from Queen Elizabeth I) and Mace reversed in token of surrender. He offers the hilt of the sword to the sovereign, who touches it and returns it. The Lord Mayor and Aldermen then precede the monarch into the City. The ceremony symbolizes the overlordship of the sovereign at all times. Within the City, the Lord Mayor takes precedence over everyone but the sovereign.

In 1348 the City, like the rest of the country, fell victim to the Black Death, which is thought to have killed as many as half its residents. Indeed, the City experienced a long-term loss of population after the Black Death, recent research suggesting that it had fewer inhabitants in 1500 than in 1300. It seems to have suffered a major economic recession during this time, but remained, nevertheless, one of the leading cities of northern Europe and by 1600 its population had fully recovered in number.

The City's creative financial role gathered strength in the 16th century. It was the age of merchant venturers who risked their lives in an effort to find new sea trade routes and develop foreign markets. The Muscovy Company, capitalized by the City, was incorporated by royal charter. In 1533, Richard Chancellor led an expedition of three ships to find a north-east passage to Cathay. After many months of appalling privation, Chancellor found himself in Russia, at the court of Ivan the Terrible. Ivan was impressed by his uninvited visitors, and offered them a treaty giving freedom of trade to English ships, as well as a proposal of marriage to Queen Elizabeth. Soon there were other such companies, including the East India Company (incorporated in 1600), as trade followed the flag, backed by the merchants of London.

At the beginning of the 17th century many wealthy courtiers left the City for the new developments such as Covent Garden to the west. The merchants and tradesmen who remained were further united by their resentment of the constant demands for money which had continued under the Stuart kings. Most of the City supported Parliament during the Civil War (1642-8), an important factor in the King's defeat, as well as an attempt to reassert the City's independence.

Three other important events helped to shape the City and its role during the 17th century. The Great Plague killed as many as 100,000 Londoners over a period of eighteen months, at the rate (in September 1665) of at least 1,000 a day. No sooner had the Plague abated than the Great Fire of 1666 broke out. It burned for four days and destroyed nearly 400 acres within the City walls (and 63 acres outside), including 87 churches, 44 livery halls and 13,200 houses. Fortunately, only eight

An idealized picture of 1616 showing a sermon being preached from the open-air pulpit of Paul's Cross in the churchyard of the old cathedral.

Contemporary woodcut of the Great Fire of September 1666.

or nine lives were lost, but for the diarist Samuel Pepys it was 'the saddest sight of desolation that [he] ever saw'. Both Sir Christopher Wren and John Evelyn made schemes for redevelopment, along the lines of an Italian city with piazzas and wide streets on a grid pattern. Evelyn wanted a quay along the river, while Wren favoured a canal based on the Fleet river, but wished to exclude 'noisy trades' from the City. Both plans were turned down as 'unsuitable for a commercial city', and the extensive rebuilding was carried out largely on the basis of immediate practicality.

The third, eminently constructive, event was the establishment of the Bank of England in 1694 by William Paterson, a Scot and a member of the Merchant Taylors' Company. The goldsmiths and owners of other banks recently founded in the City were opposed to a national bank. It was, however, incorporated in 1694 by a charter from the government, rather than the king, given in return for a loan to help fight the French.

During the 17th century the trading role of the livery companies declined somewhat, although they survived as institutions. For more than 200 years after 1709 no new companies were founded but since 1932 a further twenty have been granted livery. They include the Air Pilots and Navigators, Actuaries, Accountants, and, on 17 November 1986, the Worshipful Company of Environmental Cleaners.

11

GUILDHALL

Guildhall has been the centre of London's civic government for centuries. The medieval Great Hall, with its 15th-century Gothic porch interior, is now the meeting place of the Court of Common Council and of the Livery in Common Hall, as well as the venue for many ceremonial occasions, while the surrounding buildings house the offices of the City's administration. These were rebuilt after the devastation of the Second World War, when the Corporation also took the opportunity to create a spacious courtyard or Venetian piazza, worthy of Guildhall's historical and architectural importance.

The restored medieval Guildhall.

The Guildhall's extensive crypt.

There seems to have been a Guildhall on the site since the reign of Edward the Confessor in the 11th century. The present Guildhall, although now much restored, was originally built in the 15th century, when an Alderman speaks of 'an olde and lytell cottage' being replaced in 1411 by 'a fayre and goodly house'. The building was completed in the 1430s. Underneath it is the largest medieval crypt in London, with a fine vaulted ceiling, together with a second crypt which may have been beneath an earlier Guildhall.

The huge Great Hall measures approximately 46 × 15 m. (151½ × 48 ft.), and is watched over by the limewood carvings of the giants Gog and Magog, who represent the legendary Trojan invasion of London. In the roof hang the banners of the twelve principal livery companies, the original source of much of the city's wealth and prosperity.

Many distinguished people have come to Guildhall, to be honoured by the conferment of the freedom of the City, as guests at a Lord Mayor's Banquet, or to attend one of the receptions held in honour of visiting royalty and statesmen. Others have been brought here for less happy reasons: since Guildhall was the largest hall in London after Westminster Hall, it was sometimes used for state trials.

In the 16th century, Anne Askew was brought to be tried for heresy, and Archbishop Cranmer for treason. The young Earl of Surrey (1517–47), a better poet than politician whose hot temper made him many enemies, was also arraigned for treason. He had promoted the claim of his father, the Duke of Norfolk, to be the rightful Regent to the young

Standard measures of length were installed in the Guildhall in 1878.

King Edward VI, and a plot was suspected; yet the actual charge against him was that he had quartered the arms of Edward the Confessor with his own. He was found guilty and executed on Tower Hill, scene of many beheadings.

Lady Jane Grey (1537–54), hailed as queen (which she never wanted to be) for nine days after Edward VI's death, was also brought to trial at Guildhall. A brilliant scholar, she spoke and wrote Latin and Greek and understood Hebrew and Arabic. However, the City decided to recognize Mary Tudor as queen, and Jane, with her ambitious husband Lord Guildford Dudley, was found guilty of high treason. They too lost their heads at the Tower. She was only 16 years old when she died.

In 1663 Samuel Pepys was invited to a 'grand dinner' paid for by the Lord Mayor and Sheriffs. He found it 'very unpleasing that we had no napkins nor change of trenchers and drunk out of earthen pitchers and wooden dishes'.

William Pitt, Prime Minister for the second time, broken in health but relieved by the recent victory at Trafalgar from the fear of Napoleon's invasion, was a guest at the Lord Mayor's Banquet in 1805. The Lord Mayor, Alderman James Shaw, called him 'the saviour of Europe'. Pitt's reply was modest: 'I return you many thanks, my Lord Mayor, for the honour you have done me; but Europe is not to be saved by any single man. England has saved herself by her exertions, and will, I trust, save Europe by her example.'

Sir Winston Churchill came to Guildhall in 1943 to receive the honorary freedom of the City. This was presented to him in a casket which could be used as a cigar-box and was made from oak salvaged from the bomb-damaged roof. He returned in 1955 to see Oscar Nemon's statue of himself unveiled. 'I regard it as a very high honour', he said, 'that the City of London should decide to set up a statue of me in this famous Guildhall which I have so often visited and spoken in during the last fifty years or more.'

In the Great Hall are several other monuments to national figures whose achievements have been outstanding: to Admiral Lord Nelson, with Britannia and Neptune grieving at his death; to the Duke of Wellington; to William Pitt, Earl of Chatham; and William Pitt the Younger, with Apollo and Mercury to symbolize his talents; and – earliest and most parochial – to Lord Mayor Beckford, portrayed remonstrating with George III. There are three war memorials, one to soldiers of the Royal Fusiliers (City of London Regiment) who died in the South African War (1899–1902), the others (in the porch) to a member, sons of members and officers of the Corporation of London who fell in the First World War and to a Sheriff and staff who died as a result of enemy action in the Second World War. Next to the Royal Fusiliers memorial is a 15th-century window believed to have survived from the original 1411 Guildhall.

Guildhall has twice escaped total destruction: first in the Great Fire of 1666, when the original roof and interior were lost, and then in the air raids of 1940–1. Looking at the rubble of the collapsed roof on the floor of the Hall in 1941, the architect Sir Giles Gilbert Scott was astonished to note that 'the medieval portions of the Old Hall were intact and practically uninjured'. Those ancient walls had seen the election of every Lord Mayor since 1439.

Guildhall after the destruction of the timber roof in December 1940.

THE MAYORALTY

Even people who know little else about the City have heard of its Lord Mayor. The Lord Mayor of London is head of the City of London Corporation and Chairman of its two governing bodies, the Court of Aldermen and the Court of Common Council. Among other offices, he is also Chief Magistrate of the City, and Admiral of the Port of London.

It is a demanding job. He or she is host, sometimes at the Government's request, to distinguished foreign visitors. He is goodwill ambassador for Britain whenever he travels abroad. 'At home', an ex-Lord Mayor remembers, 'he may, in one day, visit a hospital, a school, plant a tree of remembrance somewhere, open a road safety campaign or an exhibition, attend a luncheon, a trial, and a State banquet, changing his ceremonial dress several times.' In one year he may have to make as many as 350 prepared speeches, and perhaps a further 200 impromptu. Each Lord Mayor also takes the opportunity to support a favourite charity during his mayoralty.

All candidates for civic office in the City, including those for the mayoralty, must be freemen of the City of London. This is also a condition of admission to the livery of a company. Historically the freedom of the City could be obtained in one of four ways: by servitude (apprenticeship to a freeman), patrimony (descent from a freeman), redemption (purchase with the approval of the Court of Aldermen or Court of Common Council), or presentation (bestowal as an honorary gift in recognition of exceptional service). Any British subject or Commonwealth citizen over the age of 21 can be nominated for admission to the freedom of the City. The nomination is submitted to the Court of Common Council for approval.

An alderman is elected to represent each of the twenty-five wards (the City's ancient electoral districts). This office used to be held for life, but aldermen now retire at the age of 70. Aldermen are in turn eligible to become one of the two Sheriffs elected annually on Midsummer Day, and those who have served as Sheriffs are eligible for election as Lord Mayor. Sheriffs and candidates for the mayoralty are both chosen on different occasions by the Livery in Common Hall: on certain days the 23,000 liverymen of the City are summoned by their livery companies to attend Guildhall, when they form the electoral body known as Common Hall.

Election of the Lord Mayor takes place on Michaelmas Day (29 September) when the serving Lord Mayor and his entourage, carrying posies of old English flowers, go first to St Lawrence Jewry, the Corporation church, to seek guidance, and then to Guildhall where the liverymen are assembled. The Livery in Common Hall have chosen two candidates, whose names are read out and the Aldermen retire to elect one of them. They return, announce their choice, and the Lord Mayor-elect is invested with the chain he wore as Sheriff.

In October the Aldermen and High Officers go with the Lord Mayor-elect to meet the Lord Chancellor, representing the Queen, who conveys the royal approval of the appointment. On the Friday before the second Saturday in November, the Lord Mayor-elect is admitted to office in Guildhall. At the ceremony, known as the Silent Change because the two people concerned say nothing, the outgoing

The summoning of the Livery in Common Hall is attended by livery company officers in traditional costumes.

The ceremony of the Silent Change in Guildhall.

The new Lord Mayor on the balcony of the Mansion House during the Lord Mayor's Show.

Lord Mayor surrenders his insignia of office to his successor. He is now known as the *late* Lord Mayor and is said to have 'passed the chair'.

On the following day the new Lord Mayor goes in procession to the Royal Courts of Justice in the Strand, just beyond the City limit. There he is presented to the Judges of the Queen's Bench Division headed by the Lord Chief Justice and promises faithfully to perform his mayoral duties. This procession is the famous 'Lord Mayor's Show', in which the new Lord Mayor shows himself to the citizens of London as he rides through the streets in his golden coach, built in 1757. The coach is drawn by six magnificent shire horses, which weigh about a tonne each, and have splendid names like Pomp and Circumstance and Pride and Prejudice. The Lord Mayor is accompanied by soldiers, sailors, airmen, military bands and the Honourable Artillery Company (HAC), reputedly the oldest regiment in Britain and the senior regiment in the Territorial Army. A section of the HAC, dressed as pikemen and musketeers of 1641, when the Civil War began, acts as the Lord Mayor's bodyguard on ceremonial occasions.

A spectator at the Lord Mayor's Show prepares to take pictures.

Some of the many floats taking part in the procession during the Lord Mayor's Show.

From 1422 the Lord Mayor's Show usually took the form of a water pageant on the Thames, with the magnificent silver-oared mayoral barge as its centrepiece. This tradition ended in 1856 when the Corporation ceased to be responsible for Thames conservancy. Some of the Victorian shows, in the heyday of the Empire, were spectacular. The theme for 1850 was Britannia, complete with camels and elephants, saluting the world (much of which she ruled) and offering peace to all continents. In 1876 elephants and their mahouts again stole the show, the turbans just clearing the arch of Temple Bar which then stood at the entry to Fleet Street. The present shows contain a pageant

The sumptuous 18th-century red and gold coach of the Lord Mayor with allegorical paintings by the Italian artist Cipriani set in the panels.

18

on the Lord Mayor's 'theme': a particular industry, a good cause, or a topic of national or international importance. In 1981 Sir Christopher Leaver chose 'Transport', and in 1983 Dame Mary Donaldson, the first woman Lord Mayor, chose 'It's People that Matter'. The numerous floats, sponsored by the livery companies and other City interests, are colourfully decorated, and the show is a popular outing for the thousands of spectators who line the streets.

On the Monday following the Show, the Lord Mayor's Banquet is held at Guildhall. This annual event, given in honour of the old Lord Mayor rather than the new one, dates back more than four centuries. A remarkable cross-section of people attends: the Prime Minister and Cabinet Ministers, representatives of the Commonwealth and foreign countries, leaders of Church and State, commerce and industry, members of the diplomatic corps and armed forces, and judges in their robes. The Lord Mayor in his black and gold robe and the Lady Mayoress with her Maids of Honour welcome their distinguished guests in the Old Library of Guildhall, to the accompaniment of a fanfare of trumpets. As they walk round the Great Hall to take their seats for the banquet, a band in the gallery plays a march from Handel's *Scipio*.

After dinner the proceedings are broadcast to the nation. The Lord Mayor proposes a toast to Her Majesty's Ministers and in replying the Prime Minister reviews the national and international situation in a major policy speech. The evening ends with the Archbishop of

An illustration from The Graphic, *1876, showing elephants passing under the old Temple Bar in the Lord Mayor's Show of that year.*

Canterbury toasting 'the Lord Mayor and the Court of Aldermen' and thanking the Lord Mayor and Sheriffs for their hospitality.

The Lord Mayor entertains many guests at Mansion House, which is his official residence during his term of office. The Lord Mayor's need of an official residence became clear in the late 17th and early 18th centuries. A competition for the design of the building was held in 1735 and was won by George Dance (the Elder), Clerk of the City Works. His Mansion House is a palatial building in the Palladian style, and includes a ballroom, a banqueting room, and accommodation for the household staff as well as for the Lord Mayor and his family. By 1752, after fifteen years' work, the building was sufficiently complete for the then Lord Mayor, Sir Crisp Gascoyne, to move in. The whole project, including the furniture, had cost more than £75,000.

The most important room in the Mansion House is probably the Egyptian Hall, with its impressive barrel ceiling. The ceiling is a later addition. Originally there was an extra storey above it nicknamed Noah's Ark, but this decayed and was replaced in 1795 by the present lower roof. There are a number of other richly decorated state apartments as well as the Lord Mayor's offices and private rooms. In the Salon is one of the Mansion House's most treasured possessions, a set of 18th-century armchairs presented to the Lord Mayor by London's citizens in memory of Nelson's victory at the Nile in 1797. A more recent gift to the Lord Mayor was a gold-coloured telephone, the millionth instrument connected in the London telephone area.

The first of the Lord Mayor's three household officers is the Swordbearer, who is the senior of his esquires. On ceremonial occasions he wears a hat of beaver fur and bears the State Sword. Second is the Common Cryer and Serjeant-at-Arms. The Common Cryer bears the Mace and calls for silence in Common Hall with the words 'Oyez, oyez, oyez. You good members of the Livery ... draw near and give your attendance.' The third household officer is the City Marshal who 'controls the marshalling of most civic processions and calls the names of the members thereof in their proper order.' All three, with the guidance of the Lord Mayor's Private Secretary, assist in the administration of the Lord Mayor's engagements and attend him in rotation on his daily rounds of duty.

The Lord Mayor's title has changed over the centuries. In the 13th century he was referred to in Latin as *dominus maior*, from which came the title mayor. The first reference to a Lord Mayor was in 1414, and by 1500 it was in general use.

The City has had a great variety of Lord Mayors, most of them worthy, a few of them notorious. It is now usual for the Lord Mayor to serve only one year in office, but Fitz-Ailwyn, the first mayor, is said to have held the post for twenty years. In the early 14th century Hamo de Chigwell was elected four times and several others have served for two or three terms. The most famous Lord Mayor is probably Richard (now usually known as Dick) Whittington, who is often credited with three mayoralties. He was elected three times but actually served as mayor four times between 1397 and 1419: he was first appointed by Richard II because his predecessor, Adam Bamme died in office (as have twenty-three others). According to later legend, Whittington was a poor boy who came to the City with his cat to seek fame and fortune. He is said to have heard the sound of Bow Bells ringing 'Turn again, Whittington, Lord Mayor of London' when he was leaving in despair. Whittington may have had a cat, but he was certainly not poor. He was a son of Sir William Whittington of Pauntley in Gloucestershire and

The Egyptian Hall in the Mansion House. The magnificent stained glass window is one of two executed by Alexander Gibbs in 1868.

became a rich mercer in London. He lent money to both Henry IV and Henry V, who put him in charge of financing the completion of Westminster Abbey. He also rebuilt Newgate Prison, 'which before was a miserable dungeon'. He was a very good and generous Lord Mayor. When he died he left money for repairing St Bartholomew's Hospital, and £35 for paving Guildhall with Purbeck stone, among many other bequests in his will.

William Beckford, who served in 1762 and 1769, attacked George III's policy towards the American Colonies: he was one of several Lord Mayors who saw fit to criticize the monarchy. Notorious Lord Mayors include the scandalous John Wilkes (1774), who somehow earned the friendship of Dr Johnson, and was elected Alderman while still a prisoner in the Tower. A member of the disreputable Hellfire Club, he

Dick Whittington, one of the most famous and benevolent of the City's mayors, on his deathbed in 1423.

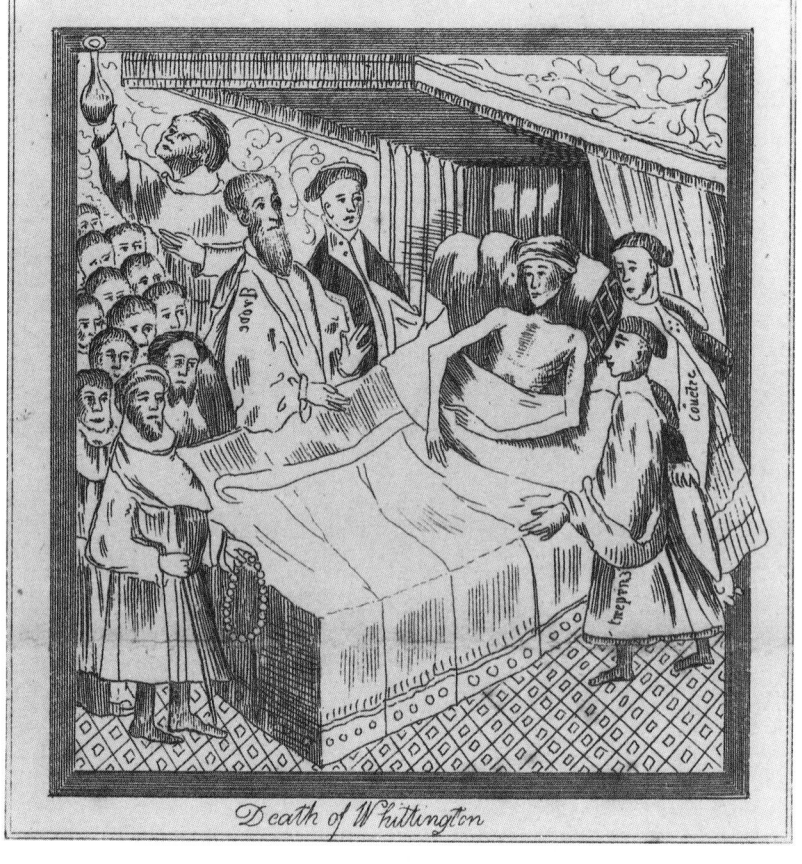

John Thomas Thorp, Lord Mayor 1820-1, holding a petition on behalf of Newgate prisoners condemned to death. He is wearing his mayoral robes over old-fashioned full court dress.

was nevertheless a reformer and a sturdy fighter for the freedom of the press. His elder brother Israel migrated to America and became the grandfather of Admiral Charles Wilkes the explorer. The Lord Mayor in 1779 was Brackley Kennett, whose wealth was partly derived from brothel-keeping.

There were two Lord Mayors in 1770, Barlow Trecothick (an Anglo-American, whose mother was a Bostonian) and Brass Crosby. It is said that Trecothick lasted only four months because of his meanness. Crosby, another champion of the press, went to the Tower for his beliefs. When he was released the City welcomed him home with pealing church bells and a 21-gun salute. To this man from Stockton-on-Tees we owe the fact that parliamentary speeches are reported verbatim and not edited by the party in power.

William Curtis, an anti-litter campaigner who fined himself five shillings for failing to keep the footpath clean outside Mansion House, was elected in 1795. He was followed by Sir Brook Watson, ex-Royal Navy, the only one-legged Lord Mayor (his other leg was bitten off by a shark at Havana, an incident commemorated in John Copley's painting in the Boston Museum of Fine Arts).

The most negligent Lord Mayor was probably Sir Thomas Bloodworth in 1666. When called out by the parish constable to deal with the Great Fire, he failed to take the matter seriously and went back to bed. The King told Samuel Pepys to order the Lord Mayor to take charge and pull down houses to prevent the fire from spreading, but by then it was too late.

ADMINISTERING THE SQUARE MILE

The Court of Common Council has been the City's main governing body for more than two centuries. Established as an elected representative assembly in 1384, today it has taken over many of the functions of the Court of Aldermen. The Council is composed of the Lord Mayor, who presides over its meetings, twenty-four other Aldermen, and 133 Common Councilmen. Residents and property-owners or tenants in each of the twenty-five City wards elect

The Court of Common Council in session in Guildhall.

A Corporation lorry sands the road in preparation for the Lord Mayor's Show.

a number of freemen, in proportion to the size of the ward, to represent them as Common Councilmen. These annual elections take place at a Wardmote on the first Friday in December.

The Court of Common Council meets every third Thursday at 1 o'clock in Guildhall. Forty members, including two Aldermen, must be present to constitute a quorum, and of these, one must be either the Lord Mayor or his *locum tenens* (an Alderman who has already been Lord Mayor). The meetings are accompanied by traditional ceremonial. The Lord Mayor sits as if enthroned in the centre of a semicircle of seats on the dais. The remaining seats in the semicircle are taken by the Aldermen. At a long table in front of the Aldermen sit the City officers, while the Commoners are seated below the dais in the body of the Court. The Sword, Mace, and Cap of Maintenance lie on a small table at the centre front of the dais, watched over by the Swordbearer and Common Cryer.

The Lord Mayor opens the proceedings with the Corporation motto *Domine dirige nos* (O Lord, guide us). At the first Common Council of a new mayoralty, and on certain other ceremonial occasions, members wear mazarine gowns, and the Lord Mayor, Aldermen, and Sheriffs wear scarlet gowns. The rich blue of the mazarine gowns, whose short sleeves are fur trimmed, is said to have been the favourite colour of Cardinal Mazarin of France.

The main business of the Court of Common Council is to consider the reports of a series of committees through which the Corporation's activities are administered. The Council makes decisions on questions of policy and expenditure, submitted to them by the committees, after full discussion and debate, with the best interests of the City always the most important consideration. The Corporation is one of the thirty-three London boroughs but it is unique among local authorities in that its elected assembly is free from party politics.

The Corporation's sources of income are also unique. In addition to its income from rates, it also has two private funds, City's Cash and Bridge House Estates. The income from these two funds is largely derived from historic charitable foundations and from properties given to the City in past centuries. It is used to fund many of the City's services and activities which might otherwise be chargeable to the rate- or taxpayer.

The City is a very successful commercial area and its properties therefore have a high rateable value. As a local authority, the Corporation collects more than £400 million annually in rates, the majority from commercial organizations. Much of this income is given to other bodies within London for services such as education. Only about 15 per cent of the City's rate income is spent within the City. This money is used to fund the usual activities of a local authority, such as the provision and maintenance of housing, libraries, public health and social services, as well as a police force and upkeep of the courts (including the Old Bailey). The rates are also used to run the Barbican Centre and to fund the work of the Port Health Authority.

City's Cash finances the City's three secondary schools, as well as the Guildhall School of Music and Drama. It is used to maintain the important open spaces owned by the City outside London, and to administer Smithfield, Billingsgate and Leadenhall markets, which the City owns. City's Cash also maintains a number of important City buildings, including the Guildhall and Mansion House, and pays for the Corporation's generous hospitality and much of the ceremonial and entertainment associated with the mayoralty. The Bridge House

The eastern City skyline from Tower Bridge with the National Westminster Bank's tower rising above the Lloyd's of London building and other offices. Part of the Tower of London can be seen in the foreground.

Estates Fund is entirely responsible for building and maintaining the four City bridges – London, Tower, Southwark and Blackfriars.

In carrying out its daily business, the Corporation is served by a number of officers. Some of these, such as the Town Clerk, City Surveyor, City Engineer, City Planning Officer, and Director of Building and Services have titles and functions not unlike those of other local authorities. Other officers, especially one known as the Secondary and Under-Sheriff and High Bailiff of Southwark Prothonotary,

An aerial view of the western part of the City with the dome of St Paul's Cathedral prominent in the centre of the picture. The Barbican Centre and the residential estate are to the north, and Guildhall to the east.

have titles whose meanings are less obvious. This particular officer combines the duties of five former officers. He is the Sheriffs' deputy and is chiefly concerned with ceremonial and administrative duties at the Central Criminal Court. Three other officers with historic posts are the Chamberlain, the Comptroller and City Solicitor, and the Remembrancer. All have important roles in the City's administration.

The Chamberlain of London is the Corporation's director of finance,

treasurer, and banker. He is receiver and paymaster of the City's income from all sources. As a ceremonial officer, he admits individuals to the freedom of the City and is particularly responsible for admission to the honorary freedom. Records of the Chamberlain's post date back as far as 1237.

The office of Comptroller and City Solicitor is the result of the successive amalgamation of several ancient posts over many years. His office provides the full range of legal services for the Corporation and advises all its committees and departments, as well as acting as legal adviser to the Commissioner of Police for the City of London on civil matters.

The Remembrancer holds a traditional office, dating back to Elizabethan times. He is the link between the City, the Crown, and Parliament, and holds a watching brief in Parliament for any matters affecting the City. He also promotes Private Bills for the Corporation when necessary. He arranges all the Corporation's entertainments and ceremonial – royal, national and civic – including the Lord Mayor's Show and Corporation functions at Guildhall and Mansion House.

Two legal figures who have been part of the City's constitution for centuries are the Recorder and the Common Serjeant. The Recorder, the senior of the Old Bailey judges, is adviser to the Court of Lord Mayor and Aldermen 'for their better direction in administering law and justice', and the Common Serjeant, second in precedence to the Recorder, also has a number of non-judicial duties. Both accompany the Lord Mayor on certain public and ceremonial occasions.

Despite its many historic traditions, the Corporation is always aware of the need to look to the future if the City is to maintain its place at the forefront of the financial world. The City of London Local Plan is an important statement of the Corporation's strategy as a local planning authority. It sets out the Corporation's short-term planning objectives within the context of its long-term principles and priorities. As the needs of the financial community become increasingly complex, and change with ever greater speed, so the Local Plan has had to be written in a way that made it flexible yet detailed. Its overall aim is 'to promote

Part of the Middle Temple, one of the four Inns of Court. Middle Temple Hall is Elizabethan, although much restored following bomb damage during the Second World War.

A small area of the vast dealing room at Barclays de Zoete Wedd. There are 600 dealing positions.

the continued development of the City as a leading international Financial Centre and, at the same time, to improve living, working and travelling conditions including social and leisure facilities and to enhance the environmental qualities of the City.'

Architecture, skyline, 'townscape', and historic heritage all contribute to 'environmental quality'. This quality is exceptional in the City of London and must be maintained. The size, height and design of new buildings need to be planned so that the new harmonize with the old, although they may not necessarily look the same. Indeed, contrast can be welcome and dramatically pleasing to the eye. There are some areas, however, where this is inappropriate. The conservation areas, of which there are twenty-two in the Square Mile, covering more than a quarter of its area, must be respected. Most of the listed buildings and historic streets are in conservation areas, and care is taken that their special character is not lost, or seriously damaged by new development. In certain areas views of and from St Paul's and from the Monument are protected as far as possible.

At the same time it is important that companies working in the City are provided with the accommodation they require in an era of new technology and changed trading conditions. Greater floor heights are needed, for example, to accommodate the additional cabling and ducting needed for computer and communications hardware and for air-conditioning. There is also an increased demand for large dealing rooms with column-free floor areas, in response to the changing patterns of trading within the City since 'deregulation'. These needs often cannot be met within existing office buildings, and many postwar buildings are being redeveloped, including many of the 1960s office blocks along London Wall. The pressure for floor space is spreading from the heart of the City to traditionally peripheral areas such as Fleet Street and Finsbury Circus, and is leading to dramatic changes in the appearance of the City.

Sometimes these two sets of aims will clash, but many international companies value the special character and heritage of the City and are

Behind the façade of the old City of London School the foundations of a new office building are being laid.

as anxious as the Corporation to preserve these qualities. They welcome the opportunity to site their new offices behind the façades of historic buildings, as has been done at the old Billingsgate Market, to give just one example. Meanwhile 'the biggest single development in the City since the Great Fire of 1666' has been built on the 10-acre Broadgate site covering part of the Liverpool Street and former Broad Street stations on the edge of the City. An extensive area of office accommodation has been provided, with shops and a circular ice-rink which can be used for open-air concerts in the summer. So the City and its planners steer a balanced path between old and new, maintaining a suitable environment for the City's continuing development and prosperity (and thus for the nation's well-being) without destroying its special and unique heritage.

THE FINANCIAL CITY

London has been an international port and centre of trade and commerce since Roman times. Banks, insurance companies and markets dealing in money and commodities have developed naturally in the area of the original centre until 'the City' became virtually synonymous with finance. Today London is one of the three most important financial market-places in the world, with New York and Tokyo. It has maintained its historical pre-eminence for several reasons: it is ideally located in the time zone between New York and Tokyo and able to deal with each at either end of the working day; it uses an international language; and, most importantly, it has shown a willingness to adapt and extend its activities to meet the rapidly changing needs of the international markets.

As a centre of international finance, the City provides a huge variety of services to other countries. These services form a major part of Britain's 'invisible exports', and earnings from them are essential in balancing the nation's budget. In the late 1980s these invisible earnings accounted for nearly half the country's foreign earnings.

Within the City, insurance is the greatest source of invisible export income. Insurance has a long history in the City. Lloyd's of London, which has a world-wide reputation, began in Edward Lloyd's coffee-house in the late 17th century. Shipowners, ships' captains, and merchants used to meet there to exchange shipping news and to arrange insurance for ships and their cargoes. Mr Lloyd made it his business to provide them with the most up-to-date information and his coffee-house became the centre for shipping insurance. *Lloyd's List*, first published as *Lloyd's News* in 1734, is still a leading source of information about shipping news and movements.

Lloyd's expanded beyond the marine insurance market in the late 19th century, and now almost anything can be insured there. It is

The interior of a City coffee-house as it might have appeared in 1763.

The central escalator rising above the trading floor inside the Lloyd's of London building, designed by Richard Rogers and opened in 1986.

unique in the way it operates. It has no shareholders but is an association of private insurers who accept individual liability for the risks they underwrite. In order to minimize the size of their liabilities, Lloyd's members group themselves into syndicates. The syndicates' underwriters cannot be approached direct by the public, but only through an insurance broker.

Banking is another City activity with a long history and a reputation for trust and integrity. The Bank of England is the government's bank,

A selection of City bank signs.

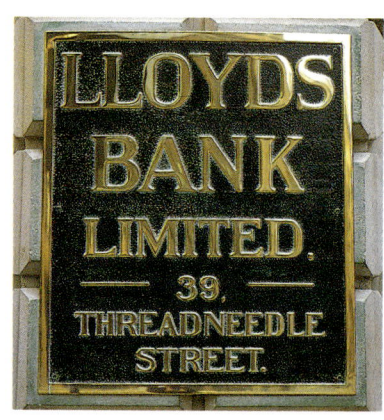

as well as the City's leading institution. Among many important roles, it manages the government's debt, borrowing money from the public and from financial institutions which enables the government to run the country, and paying interest on these borrowings. The Bank of England also issues the nation's bank notes and coins. Until 1931 the bearer of a bank note had the right to demand its exchange for the equivalent in gold from the country's reserves, which are still held in the Bank's vaults.

These notes and coins are distributed through the clearing banks, which have branches in every High Street. The 'Big Four' (Barclays, Lloyds, Midland, and National Westminster) all have their head offices in the City. The clearing banks' main function is to hold deposits and make loans, but they are probably best known to most people as a means of making and receiving payments by cheque. Between them the banks handle more than 6 million cheques a day, transferring money from one account to another.

Merchant banks are less well known to the public and their activities are difficult to define. Essentially, they finance trading and commercial enterprises, by lending money, and give advice on such matters as company take-overs and mergers. In recent years, they have diversified widely to meet the challenges of international business, and the range and scope of their dealings is formidable.

Another recent development is the rapid increase in the number of foreign banks in the City. It has been said that there are more American banks in London than in New York itself.

An important event enabling the City to maintain its position at the centre of the international financial stage was the deregulation of the Stock Exchange in 1986. The Stock Exchange has been a market-place for dealers in stocks and shares since the 18th century, and was the world's leading stock market in the 19th century. Its business used to be conducted by jobbers, who bought and sold shares on their own account and made their money from the difference between the buying and selling prices, and brokers, who bought and sold shares on behalf of their clients through a jobber, making their money by charging commission on the deal. Since deregulation the minimum commission has been abolished, together with the distinction between jobber and broker. This has led to major changes in the way the City's dealers and bankers are organized, with a great increase in competition between the big institutions. The market-makers who have replaced the old brokers and jobbers now operate from large dealing rooms, using telephones and computers to communicate with one

The trading floor of the Baltic Exchange, housed since 1903 in Edwardian marble splendour in St Mary Axe.

another, and the Stock Exchange floor has been closed. These changes are having far-reaching effects on the City's operations, but their full import is only gradually becoming clear as the markets adapt to the new dynamic atmosphere.

The City is essentially one vast market-place containing many smaller markets. In addition to the banking and insurance sectors, and the market for stocks and shares, there are a number of markets dealing in goods and commodities of various kinds. Buyers and sellers of staple items such as coffee, cocoa, sugar, and wool trade them in the commodity markets, which are administered by the London Commodity Exchange. Brokers act as intermediaries and the markets are 'open outcry': bids and offers are shouted out and deals are made verbally on the basis of trust. Other commodities are traded at the Baltic Exchange, although the Exchange's chief 'commodity' is freight. It is a market in ship and air cargo space. Much of the world's freight chartering, and the sale of about half the world's ships, is arranged here. The London Metal Exchange is the market for six metals – silver, copper, tin, zinc, lead, and aluminium – each of which is traded by open outcry in two five-minute sessions daily, by dealers seated in a ring. Gold is traded in a separate bullion market. Twice daily five members meet to fix the price. Each holds a small Union Jack, which he raises or lowers to indicate whether or not he is willing to deal at the suggested price.

Many commodities are traded as 'futures'. The seller contracts to supply a specified quantity of the commodity at a particular price on an agreed date in the future. Many of these contracts do not actually result in the delivery of goods, since the futures markets are used as a form of insurance or hedge against anticipated changes in the prices of raw materials, and are cancelled by subsequent contracts.

The newest futures markets was established in 1983 to deal in financial futures, such as interest rates and foreign currencies. It is known as the London International Financial Futures Exchange, or LIFFE (pronounced 'life'), and is yet another open outcry market. Its establishment may perhaps be symbolic of the City's own financial future, for it marks a willingness to move forward into new markets while retaining the traditions of trust and integrity which are the legacy of hundreds of years of history.

FOUR BRIDGES

The River Thames flows through the heart of London, past the City on its northern bank. A boat trip from Westminster to Tower Pier is an interesting excursion, giving a different view of familiar landmarks such as St Paul's and the Monument. The banks of the Square Mile are marked by the symbol of the dolphin, which wraps itself round the lamp posts along the Embankment, as a reminder that London is a port. Today the port has moved downstream to Tilbury and the old docklands below the Tower have been replaced by ambitious new developments.

For many centuries, until Westminster Bridge was opened in 1750, London Bridge was the only means of crossing the Thames except by boat. The hundreds of ferrymen and wherrymen always opposed the building of new bridges, so that, in order to cross the river by bridge

The Monument (1761–7), a huge Doric column of white Portland stone, was designed by Sir Christopher Wren and Robert Hooke to commemorate the Great Fire of 1666.

west of London Bridge, a detour had to be made all the way to Putney. London Bridge, the first stone bridge across the Thames, was built in the 12th century by Peter, Chaplain of St Mary Colechurch, who was inspired by God in a vision. Begun in 1176, the bridge took thirty-three years to complete. It had nineteen arches and a chapel dedicated to St Thomas à Becket, in which Peter, who died four years before the bridge was finished, was eventually buried. His bridge lasted for six centuries, accumulating shops and houses along its length, together with the heads of executed traitors impaled on spikes. Rich merchants as well as poorer people left money 'to God and the Bridge' when they died. In 1300 Joanne Bytheway left the bridge twelve pence, and a year later Marjorie Batchelor bequeathed her only possession, her wedding ring. The Trust still exists today, as Bridge House Estates. Its revenue continues to be used for the maintenance of London Bridge, at no cost to the rate- or taxpayer, as well as funding and maintaining the three other bridges owned by the Corporation: Blackfriars, Southwark, and Tower Bridge.

Blackfriars Bridge, originally built in 1760–6, had nine stone arches. Its official name was William Pitt Bridge but Londoners preferred to name it after the old Black Friars monastery (where a pub now stands). The present bridge of wrought iron and granite was opened in 1869 by Queen Victoria, accompanied by her Scottish servant, John Brown. She was so unpopular at the time that she was hissed as she rode through the streets.

The first Southwark Bridge was completed in 1819. There had been some opposition to its building because the river narrows at this point and there were fears that another bridge would obstruct shipping. John Rennie's bridge of three arches was the largest ever constructed of cast iron. It was magnificent to see, but by the 20th century it was out of date and was replaced by the present five arches of steel, opened in 1921. Harry Harris, whose family had been licensed watermen for six generations, and whose grandfather claimed to remember Old London Bridge when there were houses on it, celebrated Mafeking Night in 1900 by walking end to end along the parapet of Rennie's bridge.

Old London Bridge c.1600, drawn by John Norton, Royal Surveyor to Elizabeth I. The river was funnelled with such force through the narrow channels between the bridge's piers that many boatmen lost their lives when their boats overturned. Passengers often preferred to alight rather than risk the rapids.

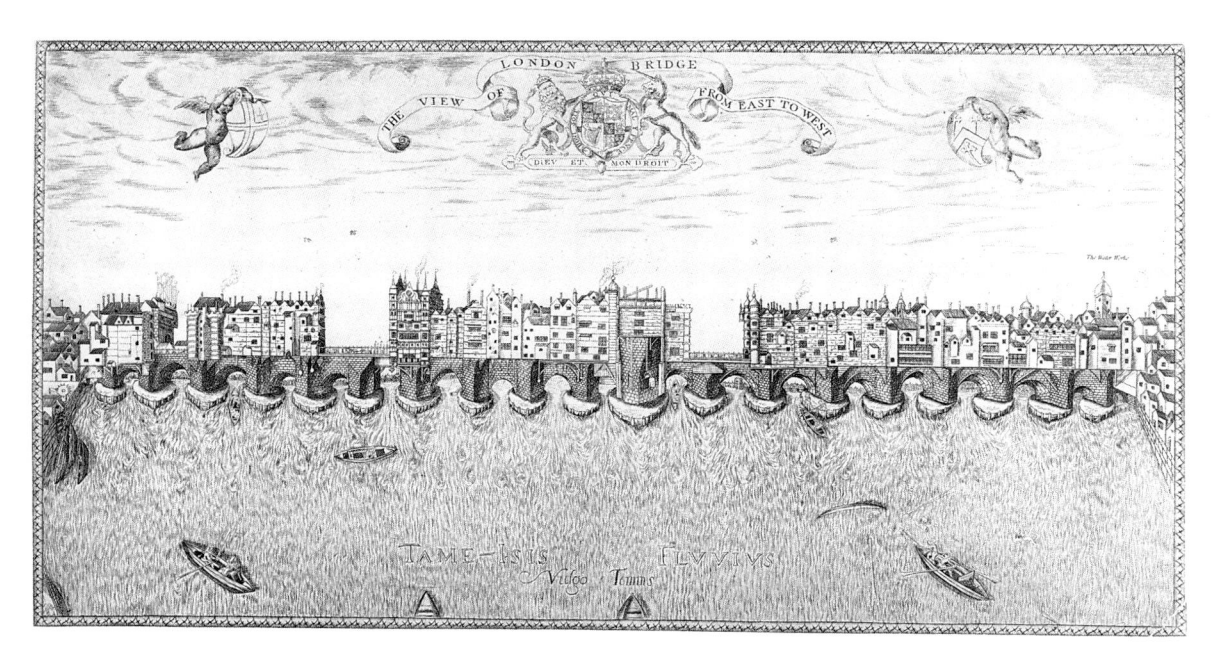

Southwark Bridge (in the background), Cannon Street railway bridge and London Bridge seen from the walkway of Tower Bridge. HMS Belfast (foreground) is a popular tourist attraction.

Peter of Colechurch's medieval London Bridge lasted until the 19th century. Its many arches obstructed the flow of the river so badly that it sometimes froze in winter and ice-fairs could be held upon it. The bridge had seen Henry V return triumphant from Agincourt, attended by the Lord Mayor and Aldermen; the heads of Jack Cade and Sir Thomas More, preserved in tar, impaled above the gatehouse; and the procession of Charles II to reclaim his throne. A new bridge of five arches, designed by the elder Rennie and built by his son a short distance upstream from the old one, was opened in August 1831 by William IV and Queen Adelaide, who were entertained to a banquet in a giant marquee on the bridge itself. This bridge lasted until 1967 when building of the present three-span bridge of pre-stressed concrete began. Rennie's London Bridge was not only too narrow and fragile for the traffic volume of the 1970s and after, but was also so heavy that it

Inside VIEW of the GRAND PAVILION, erected on NEW LONDON BRIDGE, for the reception of THEIR MAJESTIES, on its OPENING Aug. 1. 1831.

King William IV and Queen Adelaide celebrating the opening of the new London Bridge in 1831.

was slowly sinking into the river bed. The new bridge, less beautiful but more practical, weighs less than half Rennie's granite bridge. Opened by the Queen in 1973, the new London Bridge has dual three-lane carriageways and more than 12 m. (40 ft.) of pavement width. By ancient tradition freemen of the City are entitled to drive sheep across it.

The stones of Rennie's bridge were bought for £1 million by the McCulloch Oil Corporation of California, imported duty-free as 'a genuine large antique' into the United States and re-erected at Lake Havasu City, Arizona, where it links the Old World with the New and has stimulated all sorts of good-humoured Anglophilia, notably a traditional British pub, The City of London Arms, selling authentic British beer.

Tower Bridge, opened by the Prince of Wales (Edward VII) in 1894, is a beautiful anachronism, even a 'folly', which is as much a symbol of London as the Eiffel Tower is of Paris. Designed by the City Architect, Horace Jones, in Gothic style, and built by the leading civil engineer of the day, Sir John Wolfe Barry, it now attracts over 400,000 tourists a year. It used to be opened to shipping up to fifty times a day, but as the Port of London moved downstream its usefulness declined and the twin bascules (now operated by electricity) open only three or four times a week. The original hydraulic engines now form part of a museum. A large model explains how they worked and there is a display tracing the history of the City's bridges from Roman times. From the glass-enclosed walkways across the top (33.5 m./110 ft. above the road), there are panoramic views of the City, whose chief landmarks are identified. In 1952 the bascules rose while a bus was still crossing the bridge. The driver, a man of strong nerves, accelerated smartly, jumped the gap and saved both his bus and his passengers.

opposite: Tower Bridge, from the south-west.

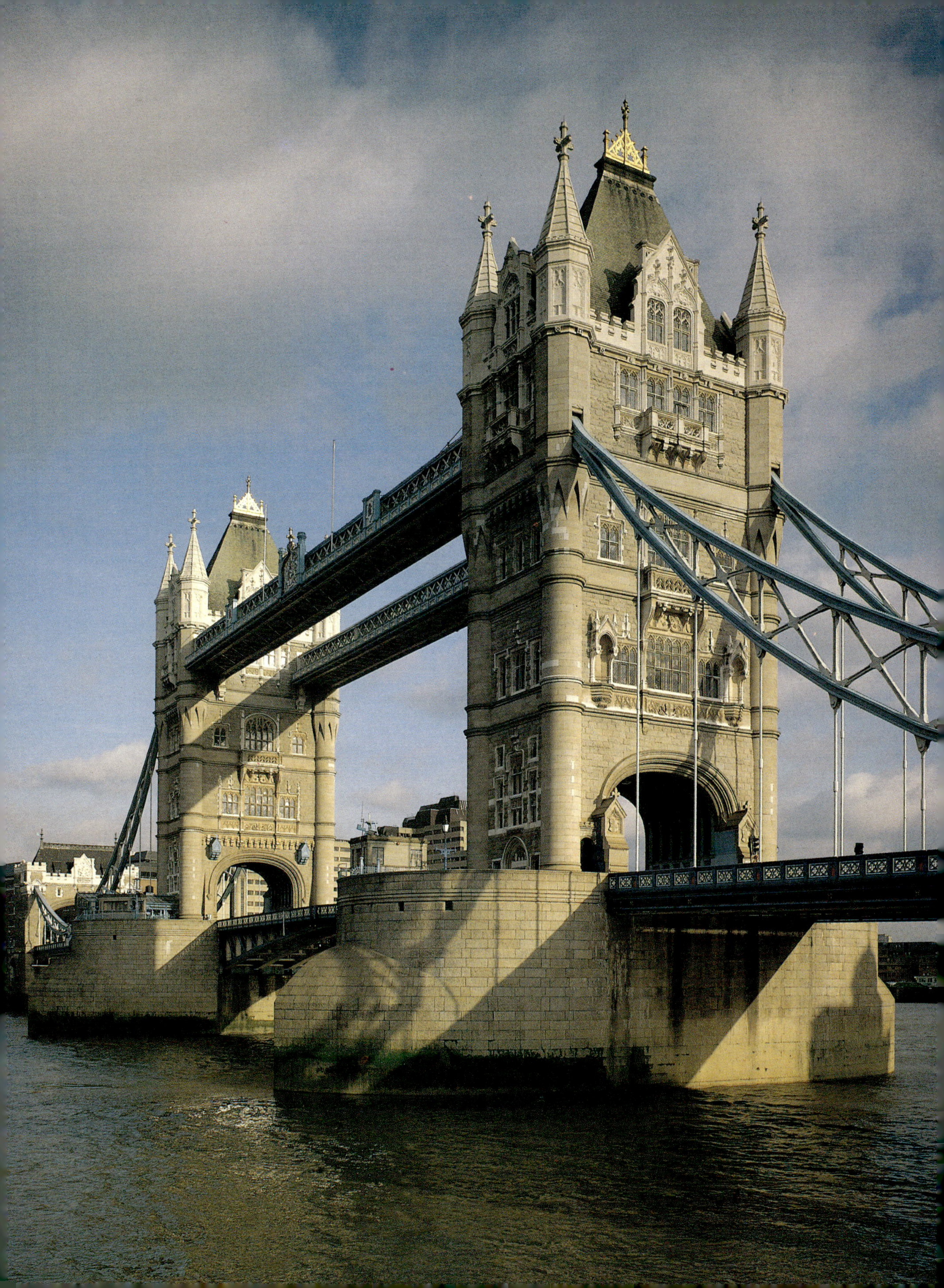

THE CITY'S HEALTH

The Registrar General's Report for December 1865 asserted: 'The importance of attention to the hygienic condition both of our merchant vessels and our seaports is clearly seen, for a foul ship, instead of merchandise, carries from land to land the seed of depopulating diseases, and a foul seaport supplies the soil in which they rankly germinate.'

London was the largest port in the world at the time and it remains by far the biggest mixed port in the country. Disease in the port could affect not only the City and the Thames Estuary but the whole country. Britain is an island, and the immediate fear in the 19th century was of a cholera epidemic raging on the Continent.

In 1872 the Corporation of London was made the 'Sanitary Authority' of the Port of London (in 1936 it became the 'Health Authority'). The first Port Medical Officer of Health was Dr Harry Leach. He was assisted by a Sanitary Inspector whose diverse range of duties included the inspection of ships. Initially these duties were restricted to vessels visiting City wharves but later his area of responsibility was extended. Soon the Corporation provided Dr Leach and the Inspector with a steam launch for their duties and the Admiralty lent the vessel *Rhin* as an isolation hospital ship. From 1883

Lithograph by William Parrott (1841) of the Pool of London from London Bridge. The Custom House (1814–26) is on the left bank, with the Tower of London in the distance.

Staff with a few of the inmates of the Animal Quarantine Station at Heathrow Airport, run by the Corporation of London.

the Corporation became responsible for the health of 60 miles of the Thames and its estuary, from Teddington Lock to Warden Point in the Isle of Sheppey, and of the lower reaches of the River Medway including the port of Sheerness. The limits were extended seaward in 1965 to include a further 34 miles of the Thames Estuary.

Today the Corporation has an enormous variety of health responsibilities. As the London Port Health Authority, these include the health of passengers and crews of vessels in the Port, the control of imported food cargoes, and of shellfish harvested from the Thames Estuary. All ships entering the Port of London are subject to strict health control. The ship's master must report (by radio) if anyone aboard his vessel appears to be suffering from symptoms suggesting an infectious disease. A team of doctors is on call at Gravesend, together with two launches, fitted out as floating ambulances, which are used for boarding incoming vessels. Some $3\frac{1}{2}$ million tonnes of food are imported annually into the Port Health sector (about a quarter of the United Kingdom's food imports enter the country through the Port of London) and many consignments are examined to ensure that they are fit for human consumption and comply with the numerous Acts and regulations currently in force. Around the Thames Estuary about 27 square miles of water provide ideal breeding grounds for molluscan shellfish, primarily cockles, and these are heat-treated to prevent the risk of illness prior to being sold for human consumption. Oysters from the River Roach in Essex are also cleansed under the supervision of the Port Health Inspectors.

Within the City the Corporation supervises food hygiene, including meat inspection at Smithfield Market, and public health matters generally. This covers drainage, health and safety for 350,000 office workers, noise and air pollution, water supply and pest control. In 1955 the City was the first authority in Britain to become a smokeless zone. This was the achievement of the Port and City of London Health Committee under the chairmanship of Mr Deputy Stanley Cohen, CBE, FRSA, who fought for many years for clean air. Even clean air seems to have a 700-year-old tradition behind it: in 1273 the use of 'sea coal' was prohibited in London, and an artificer was executed for using it in his furnace.

Of national importance are the City's veterinary services which, acting on behalf of the Department of the Environment, reach far outside the Square Mile to zoos in Bedfordshire, Kent and Surrey. The staff's duties may involve anything from supervising sheep dipping on a farm to attending television studios to ensure public safety and animal welfare when a programme features dangerous animals. The Animal Quarantine Station at Heathrow Airport was opened by the Lord Mayor in 1977. It was built and equipped by the Corporation, who now run it, and is the only one of its kind in the world. As part of its many duties carried out on behalf of the Ministry of Agriculture, Fisheries, and Food it monitors all the birds imported commercially into Britain for disease. It can hold a wide range of animals in isolation, from domestic pets to elephants, big cats and humming birds, and it handles animals which are being imported or exported via Heathrow, or are in transit through the airport. Preventive measures and the prosecution of offenders against the animal import regulations are another of the Corporation's activities. As part of the campaign against the introduction of rabies and other diseases, warning notices are displayed at airports and along the Thames, aimed at preventing the illegal landing of animals from abroad.

MARKETS: WHOLESALE AND RETAIL

Heretics used to be burnt at Smithfield. More cheerfully, Bartholomew Fair was held there from 1123 until the middle of the 19th century, when it was forbidden because of 'rowdiness and debauchery'. Today Smithfield is London's central meat market and the largest in the world. Cattle used to be driven through the streets of London to be killed at Smithfield but this practice was stopped when the Corporation opened a new cattle market at Islington in 1854. The present Smithfield Market was built as a market for dead meat by Horace Jones, the City Architect, to a design inspired by the Crystal Palace. The building was completed in 1868. The coming of railways and refrigeration, enabling meat to be imported, together with London's tremendous 19th-century population explosion, led to the addition of three further sections. The Poultry Market, built in 1872, was mostly destroyed by fire in 1958, but was rebuilt in 1963. The main meat market buildings are undergoing major refurbishment, creating an entirely modern market within the restored exterior. Trading starts at 5 a.m. and is all but completed by 9.30 a.m.

Leadenhall market was also designed by Horace Jones, in 1881. There has been a market on this site since the 14th century, and it is named after a lead-roofed mansion which stood near by at that time. Today's market is a very attractive glass-roofed building. The market used to be wholesale, concentrating on game and poultry, but it is now predominantly retail. It is a prime shopping area for meat, poultry, fish and game, with an old-fashioned atmosphere. The public houses, wine bars and eating-places under its roof make it very popular with City workers at lunch time.

Smithfield meat market during early morning trading. The 19th-century iron and glass interior is being extensively modernized.

Leadenhall market, for centuries famous for wholesale poultry and game, is now a charming retail arcade.

Billingsgate had been the site of a market from Saxon times. In 1982, however, Billingsgate Market moved from its old site near London Bridge to a new site in Docklands. This new site is leased by the Corporation from the London Borough of Tower Hamlets for a 'peppercorn' rent of suitable fish, which is distributed to old people's homes in the borough. Billingsgate is a fish market and has been so since at least 1699. Traditionally the porters wore leather hats for carrying boxes of fish but now trucks are used instead. One relic of the old market which has survived is the Billingsgate Bell, which announced the beginning of trading in the market's new home. It rings every day at 5.30 a.m. and at noon to declare the market open and closed, although most of the fish has been sold by 9 a.m. Billingsgate is now one of the most modern fish markets in the world. Its new buildings were provided by the Corporation out of City's Cash, and the

Engraving by Gustave Doré (1872) of Billingsgate porters on the quayside wearing their traditional hats for carrying heavy loads.

Corporation continues as the Market Authority, despite the move outside the City limits.

The other great City market is Spitalfields, which specializes in fruit, vegetables and flowers. Spitalfields is also just outside the City, in Tower Hamlets, but has been owned by the Corporation since 1920, when £2 million was spent on its modernization. It is a wholesale market whose essential function is to speed the supply of perishable goods in the freshest possible condition to outlets all over Britain. The market was created by royal charter in 1682, when Spitalfields was an agricultural area and the produce sold was locally grown. Beneath the market is a series of chambers used for ripening bananas.

All these markets are the special responsibility of the Corporation, who maintain their buildings, and ensure that public health regulations are complied with. These early morning markets are fascinating places to visit, with their bustle, their characters, and their extraordinary range and quality of goods. No less fascinating is Petticoat Lane, one of the City's street markets. It was called Petticoat Lane because many old clothes dealers traded there in the 17th century. Nowadays the market spills over into side streets, where you can buy everything from reptiles to furniture on Sunday mornings.

LAW AND ORDER

The 800-strong City of London Police are the sophisticated successors to the medieval 'watch and ward' (the night and day guard which manned the City's walls against attack) and the elderly 'Charlies' with lanterns and sticks who preceded Peel's top-hatted 'Peelers'. The present City police were founded by the City of London Police Act of 1839. They are distinguished from the Metropolitan Police by their Roman-type helmets, correctly termed 'comb helmets', by the gilt buttons and gold chevrons on their arms and their red-and-white armbands. The men must must all be at least 180 cm. (5 ft. 11 in.) in height, and the women 167.5 cm. (5 ft. 6in.), taller than other forces require.

They are equipped for the very specialized requirements of crime prevention and detection in a square mile of commerce and great wealth, with a large daily population but a small residential one. Burglary and theft are the most common crimes, and there are special policing problems arising out of visits to the City by foreign heads of state, royalty and other VIPs, as well as from annual events such as the London Marathon and the Lord Mayor's Show and Banquet.

Aquatint by Rowlandson, Pugin and Bluck (1809) of a London watch house. Before the creation of the police force such night watchmen were the only, and usually ineffective, safeguard against street robberies and violence.

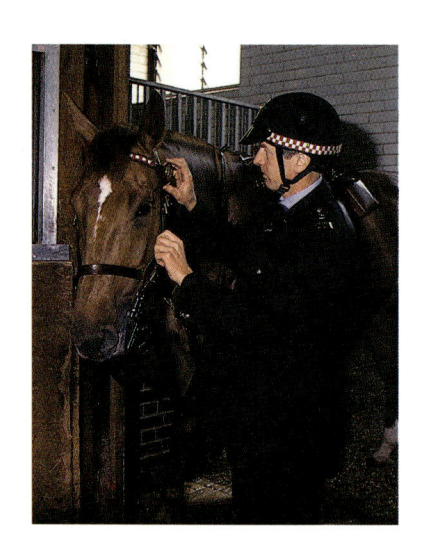

A member of the City of London's mounted police force preparing his horse for the day's work.

There are police stations at Snow Hill and Bishopsgate, with the headquarters at Old Jewry and offices at Wood Street where various departments are housed, including a small museum. There is, in addition to the CID, a Cheque Squad, a Dog Section and a Mounted Branch. Immediately after the Second World War a Company Fraud Department was set up jointly with the London Metropolitan Police. As the financial City becomes more and more international, this department's work becomes increasingly complex as it deals with cases involving millions of pounds and different currencies. Some of the newer courts at the Central Criminal Court, built by the Corporation of London, were specially designed to cope with the mass of documents such cases involve.

The Central Criminal Court is the greatest criminal court in Britain, hearing the more serious cases for the Greater London area, as well as some of the more infamous trials from outside it. The court is commonly referred to as the Old Bailey, the name of the street on which it is located. 'Bailey' is derived from the word 'ballium', used in Roman times to describe a defensive wall, a section of which was uncovered during excavations in the early 1900s. The wall ran along the east side of Old Bailey and 'Dead Man's Walk', along which condemned prisoners took their last steps to the gallows, is said to have run parallel to it. The present building, designed by E.W. Mountford and built on the site of the old (and notorious) Newgate Prison, was opened by Edward VII in 1907. It now has nineteen court rooms and seventy cells for prisoners. Its dome is surmounted by Pomeroy's famous statue of Justice, carrying her scales, whose head is 65 m. (212 ft.) above the ground. Contrary to popular belief, however, she is not blindfolded.

Although Newgate Prison has long been demolished, it is still remembered in an old custom: on state occasions the civic ceremonial party, headed by the Lord Mayor and the judges, carry posies of sweet-smelling flowers, and herbs are strewn on the ledge of the dock. It used to be thought that the flowers and herbs would ward off the stink and jail fever from the prison. Ceremony reaches its peak at the beginning of the quarterly sessions, when the Lord Mayor, accompanied by the Swordbearer, Serjeant-at-Arms and City Marshal, travels by car from the Mansion House, is met by the two Sheriffs and the Secondary, and greets the High Court judges before opening the session.

The judges of the Court include the Lord Chancellor, Lord Chief Justice, all High Court judges, Aldermen of the City of London, and the resident judges, the most senior of whom are the Recorder and the Common Serjeant. A High Court judge wears a scarlet robe and carries a folded black cap and white gloves. Resident judges all wear black, with the exception of the Recorder, who wears a red robe with a broad blue lapel.

A number of the trials held here have made legal history. In 1670 two Quakers, William Penn (who later founded Pennsylvania) and William Mead, a linen-draper, were tried for attending a seditious meeting – a Friends' Meeting House. The jury, ordered to bring in a verdict of guilty, refused to do so despite being locked up without food for two nights. They were eventually fined but petitioned Chief Justice Vaughan who ruled that jurors had the right to 'give their verdict according to their convictions'.

Many notorious murderers have been tried at the Old Bailey, including Dr Crippen in 1910, and Peter Sutcliffe (the 'Yorkshire Ripper') in 1981; and William Joyce ('Lord Haw-Haw') was tried and convicted of treason after the Second World War. At trials such as these long queues form outside for the limited number of seats in the public galleries.

There are lighter moments, however. In 1952 a rat appeared in No. 2 Court during a murder trial. Everything stopped. At length the judge, Mr Justice Hilbery said calmly, 'I will adjourn the court for ten minutes. Perhaps when the rat is caught it will be expeditiously executed.' It was. On another occasion, a woman in the public gallery of a court removed her shoe and threw it at the judge. He picked it up, examined it and remarked 'I'm sorry, this doesn't appear to be my size.'

The Lord Chancellor's department supervises the administration of justice within the Old Bailey, but it was built by the Corporation and is now maintained by it from rate expenditure. The Lord Mayor is a judge of the court *ex officio*, and by tradition the centre seat on the bench of the Old Bailey courts is left vacant for him.

The Mayor's and City of London Court is the City's County Court, and there are two magistrates' courts, at Guildhall and in the Justice Room at Mansion House. The Lord Mayor, as the City's Chief Magistrate, presides over the latter. The Mansion House is unique in being both a private residence (of the Lord Mayor) and a court of law. The Justice Room was converted from the Swordbearer's room in 1849. Beneath it are ten cells for male prisoners and one for women. The women's cell is known as 'the birdcage' and was once occupied by Emmeline Pankhurst, the suffragette.

The two Sheriffs and the Secondary in ceremonial robes to meet the Lord Mayor and his party at the Old Bailey.

THE BARBICAN CENTRE

The Barbican complex is one of the City of London's most ambitious and successful projects. A residential community in the heart of the City, it also houses a prestigious centre for the arts, and a sophisticated conference venue. It was built on a site near the old walls, north of St Paul's, which was part of a 60-acre area flattened by bombs in 1940, and named after the old word for a watchtower or gateway in a city's defences.

The replanning started in 1955 when the architects Chamberlin, Powell & Bon submitted a scheme to the Corporation of London for redeveloping 35 acres in the Barbican area. An important feature of this first scheme was a new building for the Guildhall School of Music and Drama, including a small theatre and concert hall for public performances. A year later a more ambitious idea came from the then Minister for Housing, Mr (now Lord) Duncan Sandys, in a letter to the Lord Mayor: 'I am convinced that there would be advantages in creating in the City a genuine residential neighbourhood, incorporating schools, shops, open spaces and other amenities, even if it means forgoing a more remunerative return on the land.'

opposite: *This dramatic curved building in the Barbican Centre is used for conferences. It overlooks the Sculpture Court.*

below: *Architectural model of the Barbican development scheme, with the medieval church of St Giles without Cripplegate and part of the old Roman wall incorporated within the vast pedestrian site.*

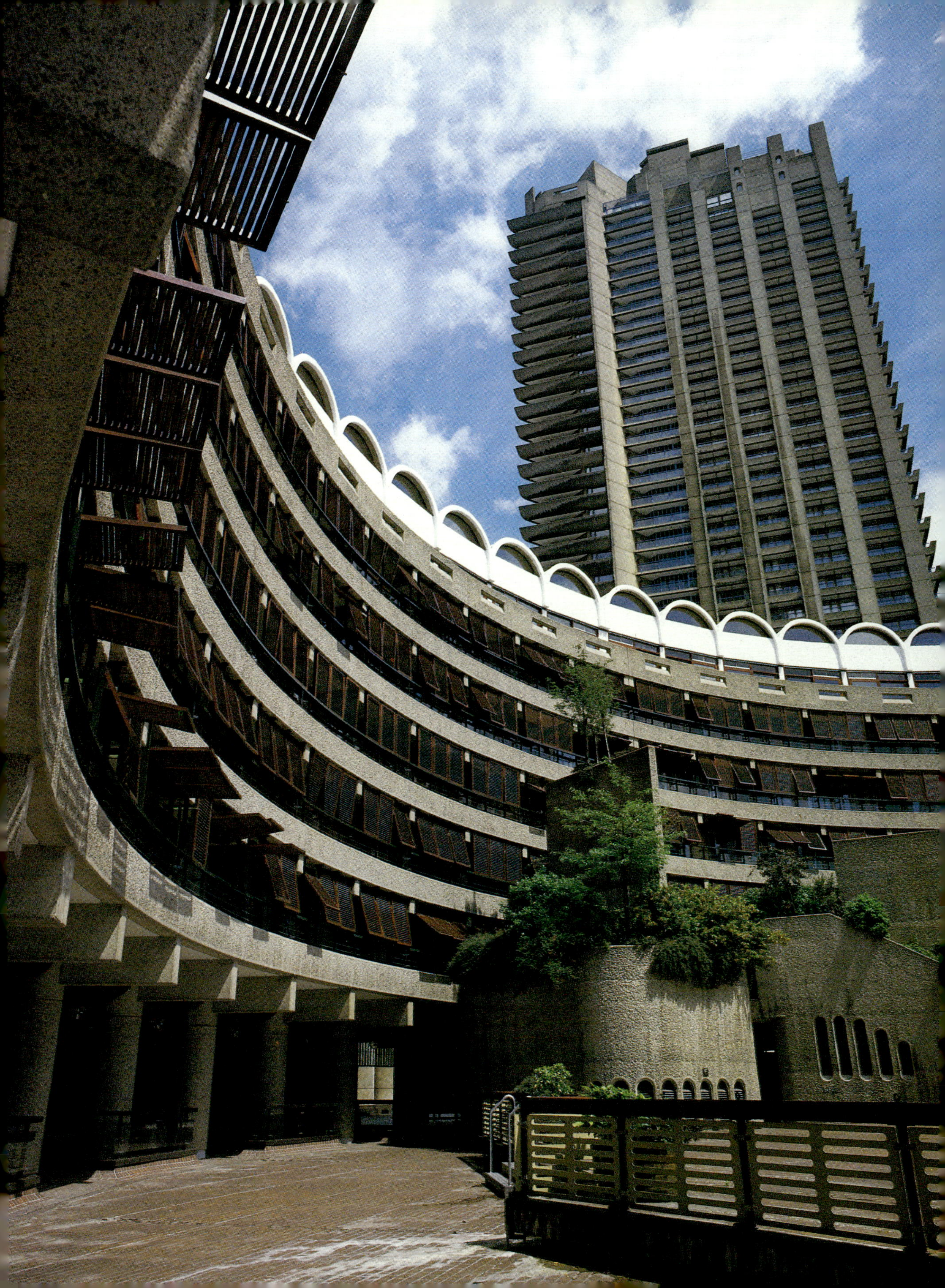

In 1957 the Barbican Committee of the Corporation was formed and by 1959 the architects had drawn up a plan which included an arts centre destined to become what has been called 'the City's gift to the Nation'. In 1964 the theatre producer Anthony Besch was asked to compile a report on how a theatre and a concert hall might be organized and managed if they were added to the plans. He recommended making permanent homes for a leading drama company and orchestra. This idea made possible a three-way collaboration between the Royal Shakespeare Company (RSC), the London Symphony Orchestra (LSO), and the Guildhall School.

A library and art gallery were added to the plans, and construction began. It became clear that the arts centre had grown too big in conception for its parts to be managed separately, and in 1970 an Administrator was appointed. In 1977 the new Guildhall School of Music and Drama opened, and on 3 March 1982, twenty-seven years after its conception, the Queen opened the completed Barbican Centre. The Centre cost £153 million to build. It was funded entirely by the Corporation of London out of City's Cash, and the Corporation continues to own, fund and manage it.

The Barbican Centre is unique. No other city can boast such a range of artistic activity under one roof. In music alone, it provides everything from solo recitals, through jazz and light entertainment, to orchestral music of all kinds, performed by musicians of international repute. The LSO presents at least seventy-five concerts annually in the 2,000-seat Barbican Hall. London's oldest orchestra, it gave its first

The Barbican concert hall, home of the London Symphony Orchestra.

concert under Dr Hans Richter, a close colleague of Wagner, at the old Queen's Hall on 9 June 1904. Richter's programme included Elgar's *Enigma Variations*, written only five years previously. The orchestra has always travelled extensively as an ambassador for British music. It toured America as early as 1912, making its first gramophone record while there. Among its many famous conductors have been Sir Henry Wood, Sir Thomas Beecham, André Previn, and Claudio Abbado.

The Royal Shakespeare Company is formed around a core of actors, directors and designers who, over years of working together, develop a distinctive approach to theatre. Its life is divided between Stratford-upon-Avon, Shakespeare's birthplace, and London. Although the works of Shakespeare are its chief concern, it also presents other classic works, together with new plays, leading to a fruitful conjunction of classical discipline and contemporary awareness.

Formed as the Stratford Memorial Theatre in 1875, the company received its royal charter in 1925. The theatre itself was built by a committee headed by Charles Flower, a local brewer, who donated the theatre's site. It opened in 1879 but was destroyed by fire in 1926. Rebuilt six years later, it is still the RSC's Stratford base. The RSC was organized in its present form by Sir Peter Hall and others at the Aldwych Theatre in 1960, moving into its new and permanent London home in 1982. Trevor Nunn, Dame Peggy Ashcroft and Peter Brook are among many other influential figures of the theatre associated with the direction of the RSC, which also occupies three small theatres: The Other Place, and the Swan (both in Stratford), and The Pit in the Barbican, which seats only 200 in a studio atmosphere.

The Centre houses an art gallery, which mounts regular exhibitions of national and international importance, covering a variety of styles and periods. The gallery also displays works of art belonging to the Corporation and other City organizations from time to time.

The largest of the Barbican's three cinemas is run as an independent repertory cinema, but it can be made available for conference use if necessary. The Barbican is a very popular venue for conferences and exhibitions. The flexible facilities offered by the purpose-built conference centre are impressive and in the evening entertainment is available on the doorstep. Conferences of up to 3,500 delegates can be accommodated in the combined space of the main hall and the five seminar rooms in Frobisher Crescent. All three cinemas, two of which are used primarily for conferences, are equipped with simultaneous interpretation facilities, closed-circuit television, film projection and sound replay systems. The Conservatory provides a very pleasant and unusual setting for coffee breaks or small receptions. It is an indoor garden area high in the roof surrounding the theatre's scenery flytower, delightfully planted with trees, shrubs and flowers.

The conference facilities are complemented by the Barbican Trade Exhibition Halls, which are adjacent to the Centre on the north side of Beech Street. The two halls are suitable for small to medium exhibitions and have been thoughtfully designed to cover exhibitors' needs.

The original purpose of the Barbican development, however, was to bring residents back to the City and this has been achieved. Its architecture may be controversial, but the Barbican Estate is a pleasant place in which to live. It was completed in 1975 and provides homes for some 3,500 people, many of whom work in the City. Accommodation ranges from bedsitting-room flatlets and maisonettes

opposite: The Conservatory, an unusual rooftop garden inside the Barbican Centre.

One of the Barbican's lakeside terraces outside the concert hall, a pleasant place to relax on a sunny day.

to luxury penthouses at the top of the three tower blocks which dominate the skyline. The residential blocks are all named after people associated with the City, such as Oliver Cromwell, who was married in nearby St Giles' without Cripplegate, and Daniel Defoe, buried in Bunhill Fields. From the upper flats of the tower blocks there are magnificent panoramic views of London and its surroundings as far as the Chiltern Hills. Shakespeare Tower is mentioned in the *Guinness Book of Records* as the tallest residential building in Britain at 123 m. (420 ft.) high.

A major advantage of high-rise building is that it liberates open space. Of the Barbican's 40 acres, 32 are open spaces, and 8 of these have been laid out as landscaped gardens including a lake. Visitors and residents alike can eat by the lake at one of the Centre's restaurants, or enjoy one of the many informal events which take place in the areas surrounding what has become the City's cultural centre, and one of the nation's most enjoyable assets.

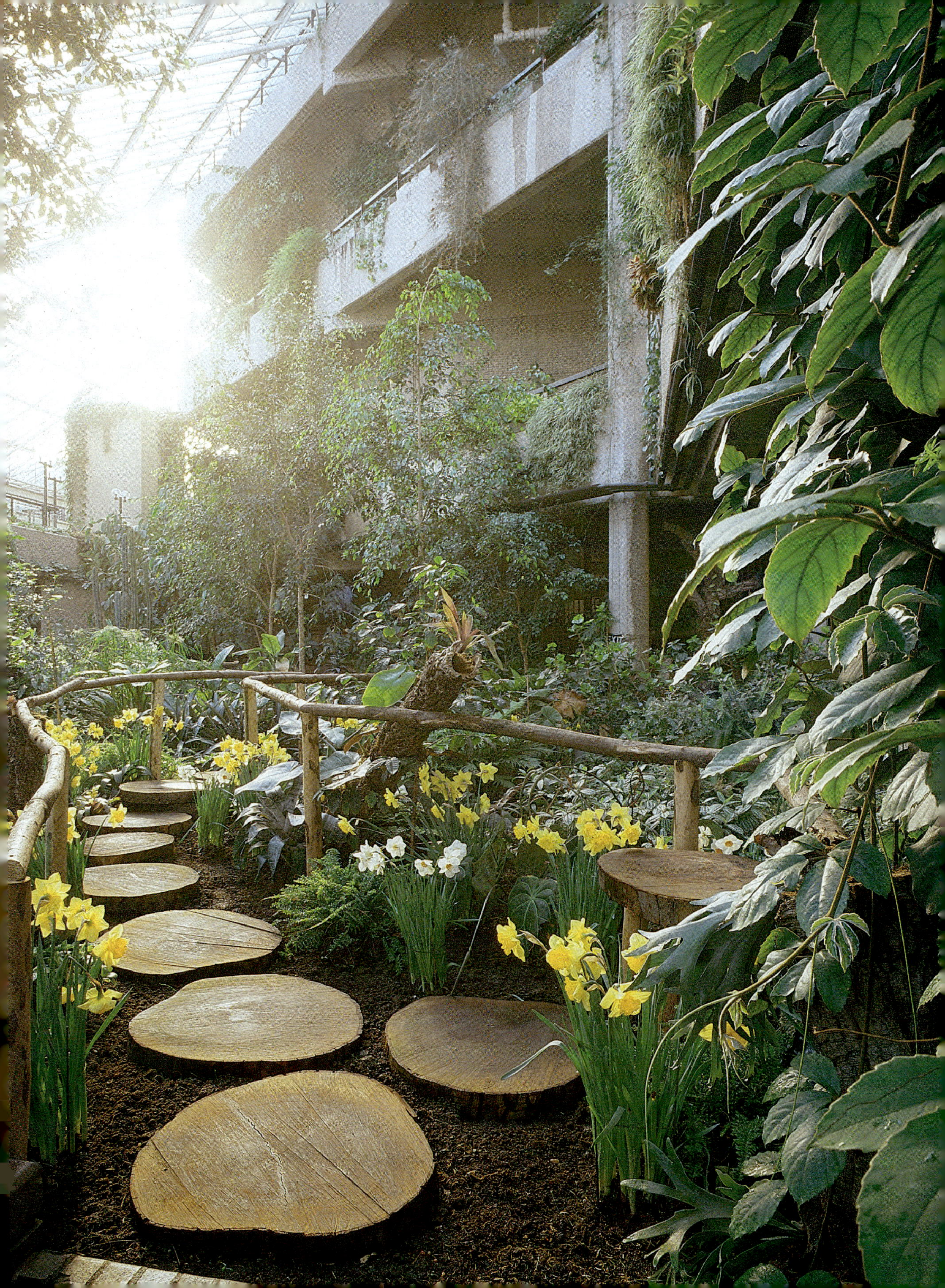

THE CITY'S SCHOOLS

The only music to be heard in medieval London outside the City's one hundred or so Norman churches was the cry of a singing watchman employed by the City fathers to reassure people that it was 'three o'clock and all's well'. In Elizabethan times, according to the Principal of the Guildhall School of Music and Drama, there were 113 different street cries for foods, trades and garments, besides that of the Common Cryer. In the 19th century ballad singers sang with equal relish of love, murder and dreadful crimes. Charles Dickens, Thomas Carlyle and their friends objected to street music because it disturbed writers at their work, and their agitation was partly responsible for the Noise Abatement Act of 1864, which regulated public noise.

For centuries, serious music could only be heard in the West End of London. Yet the first public concerts in England were given in the City in 1672 by one John Banister at his house in Whitefriars (admission one

Some of the many 17th-century street traders whose cries rang through the City.

A masterclass at the Guildhall School of Music and Drama.

shilling). Banister, a French-trained violinist, played in a string band sponsored by Charles II, but, according to Pepys, lost his job at Court because he was heard to say that English violinists were better than French.

Music was moving into the City taverns, where local people gathered to sing. One in Fleet Street specialized in string music, and the landlord began charging for seats as well as refreshment but the musicians, who ranked as 'gentlemen', soon disappeared: gentlemen could not be seen playing for money. The Worshipful Company of Musicians (or Minstrels), founded in 1500, was responsible for seeing that musical standards in the City were maintained, and had also to ensure that musicians from outside the City did not take work away from its own members.

Serious music began to return to the City in Victorian times. In September 1880 the Guildhall School of Music was opened in a humble setting, a disused warehouse in Aldermanbury, close to Guildhall. The gentleman who taught the drums is said to have given his lessons in the coal cellar. There were sixty-two students. The school seems to have developed from successful concerts given by the Guildhall Orchestral and Choral Society under the baton of Weist Hill, who became the school's first Principal. By 1887 there were 2,500 pupils and the school moved to purpose-built accommodation, designed by Sir Horace Jones, in John Carpenter Street off the Victoria Embankment. The façade proudly bore the names of five British composers, Thomas Tallis, Orlando Gibbons, Henry Purcell, Thomas Arne and William Sterndale-Bennett. By the turn of the century there were nearly 3,000 students, and full-time courses began in the 1920s.

Gradually speech and drama courses were added to the comprehensive music tuition and by 1936 a fully-fledged drama section had been established. Its reputation grew rapidly. In 1977 the school moved into its new home as 'the first denizen of the Barbican Centre for Arts and

Conferences'. The move has enabled the school to form close links with the London Symphony Orchestra and the Royal Shakespeare Company. Its equipment is the most up to date in the United Kingdom, and its tuition has few rivals. Its theatre is adapted for the training of stage management students and for the production of operas as well as plays.

Today there are over 650 full-time, and about the same number of part-time, students. The school, which enjoys university or conservatoire status, has an enviable international reputation, and the teaching staff, all working professionals, include some of the best-known performers in the United Kingdom. Solo playing, ensemble and orchestral work, acting, directing, stage design, and music therapy are all studied here.

The school has always been governed by the Music Committee of the Corporation of London. Financed out of City's Cash, it has never been a charge on rates or taxes. Its patron since 1977 has been the Lord Mayor. A random selection of students over the past century makes an impressive roll-call of talent, both serious and light: on the stage, Fred Astaire, Claire Bloom, Honor Blackman, Mrs Patrick Campbell, Noel Coward, Dudley Moore, and Sybil Thorndike; and on the concert platform, Jacqueline du Pré, Geraint Evans, James Galway, Myra Hess, Benjamin Luxon, Max Jaffa and Peter Skellern.

One of the most cheering sights occurs on Saturdays, when 'Junior Guildhall' – classes for anyone under 17 with enough talent as an instrumentalist or singer – gives extra musicianship training, the chance to take part in chamber music groups and 'workshops', and both ensemble and solo experience of performing in public. It is hard work and highly competitive, but everyone enjoys it.

John Carpenter Street, in which the Guildhall School was located until quite recently, was named after one of Dick Whittington's Town Clerks. When Carpenter died, in 1442, he left property in his will

The new riverside buildings of the City of London School, completed in 1986.

Looking out on to the playing fields of the City of London Freemen's School, which moved to Surrey in 1926.

yielding income to maintain for ever 'four boys born within the City of London who shall be called in the vulgar tongue "Carpenter's Children" to assist at divine service in the choir of the Guildhall Chapel on festival days, and to study at schools most convenient for them on ferial [non-festival] days.'

For nearly four centuries the children, by now numbering many more than four, were 'housed, fed and clothed' by the Carpenter endowment, until the accumulation of income was clearly deserving of a wider purpose. In 1834 the Corporation took over the charity and used its income 'to build and maintain in perpetuity' the City of London School. The school was built on the site of the old Honey Lane Market off Cheapside and remained there until 1882 when it moved to the Victoria Embankment. The City of London School's first great headmaster, Dr Edwin Abbott, who held the post from 1865 to 1889, was an influential scholar and educational reformer, and a founder-member, in 1870, of the Headmasters' Conference. He was instrumental in establishing the school's high academic reputation, which continues to the present day. Among many famous old boys are Prime Minister H.H. Asquith, the critic and biographer Sir Sidney Lee, the physician Lord Evans, several writers including Kingsley Amis, and Mike Brearley the cricketer.

The school's sister establishment, the City of London School for Girls, was founded in 1894, on a bequest by Mr William Ward, whose will provided £20,000 for the 'religious and virtuous education of girls'. It occupied buildings in Carmelite Street, off Fleet Street, until 1969, when it was rebuilt in the Barbican. It is next to the old church of St Giles' without Cripplegate, whose Rector allows the school to use the church on special occasions.

The Corporation of London also governs a co-educational school, the City of London Freemen's School. It began in 1854 as a school for the orphans of freemen, in Brixton, south London, which was then almost a village. As time went on, there were fewer orphans requiring free places. In 1926 the school moved to Ashtead Park in Surrey and became a fee-paying school, dropping the word 'orphan' from its name. Many freemen send their children to it as fee-paying day or boarding pupils but orphans are still admitted as Foundationers.

CITY LIBRARIES

In the early 1420s the original Guildhall Library was founded under the wills of Dick Whittington and William Bury. It became probably the first public library to be funded by a local government authority. John Stow, the 16th-century London historian, in his famous *Survey of London* (a copy of which may be seen in the present library) calls it 'a fair library furnished with books pertaining to the Guildhall'.

Unfortunately, in the mid-16th century the so-called Lord Protector, the Duke of Somerset, helped himself to the entire contents of the library, both books and manuscripts, presumably to furnish Somerset House. Today the library contains only one book known to have belonged to the original collection, a metrical translation of the Bible by Petrus of Riga. The City had to wait until 1824 for a new Guildhall Library. It was refounded at Guildhall as a library for 'the study of London, Southwark, Middlesex and parts adjoining'. In the 1870s this was replaced by a new building in Basinghall Street designed by the then City Architect, Sir Horace Jones, in perpendicular Gothic. The basements below were later used as book stores. It grew rapidly, covering many subjects beyond its speciality, the history of London, and is now one of the largest public reference libraries in London.

In August 1974 the library moved into its new and splendidly equipped air-conditioned home in the western wing of the Guildhall reconstruction scheme. The manuscript collection was moved entirely underground through the crypts of Guildhall to the strongrooms of the new building. The move took eight weeks. In the Reading Room, which is carpeted and lit from above by natural light, are the major printed sources for London history and a comprehensive quick-reference collection. The Print Room contains about 40,000 maps and 60,000 prints and illustrations, mostly of London, while the manuscript collection in the basement has extensive archives of local City bodies, including those of most City parishes and livery companies. Some of the library's most valuable special collections are kept securely in the Whittington Room.

The Reading Room of Guildhall Library, a peaceful haven for study in the modern west wing of the Guildhall.

A page from the Liber Horn manuscript of c.1311, one of the valuable collection of illuminated manuscripts in the City's Records Office.

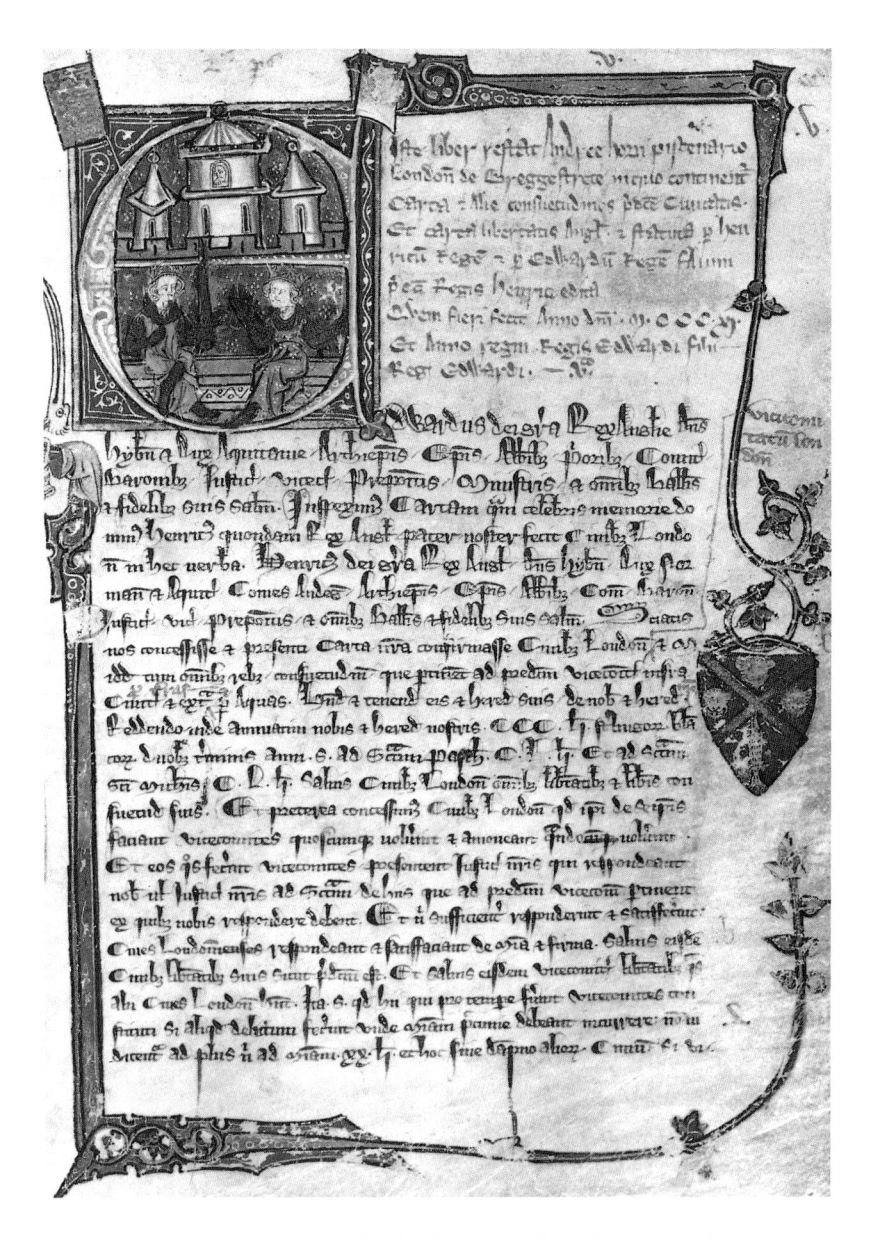

Near the entrance is the Clock Museum of the Worshipful Company of Clockmakers, one of the most important horological collections in the country, which has been on display in Guildhall Library since 1873. The company was founded by royal charter in 1631 'to regulate the craft of clock and watch making within the City of London and ten miles beyond'. Both the museum and its library were originally used for training apprentices.

Among the many treasures of the Guildhall Library is an almost complete set of London court guides and commercial directories from 1677 onwards. These list the names, addresses and occupations of London's citizens and businesses over the centuries. They are a major source of reference for London's social and economic history and are among the library's most frequently consulted documents. The library also houses one of the only six known signatures of Shakespeare; the Great Chronicle of London; the 14th-century Missal of St Botolph,

The Clock Museum, housed in Guildhall Library, records the long history of the City's clock- and watchmaking trades.

Aldersgate, with its early manuscript music and famous crucifix; the Chronicles of France (a magnificently illustrated 14th-century manuscript); and a very rare first edition of Sir Thomas More's *Utopia*. The library runs an enquiry service in English and London history, topography, genealogy and heraldry.

The City Business Library in Basinghall Street is a specialized reference library which grew out of the commercial section of Guildhall Library and was separately housed in 1970. It is a resource centre of national importance for business subjects, finance, statistics and economics. It has a wide selection of UK and foreign financial newspapers and magazines and its collection of current commercial directories is second to none.

The Libraries, Art Galleries and Records Committee of the Corporation of London runs three lending libraries, one in the Barbican and two others in Shoe Lane and in Bishopsgate to serve the Fleet Street area and the eastern part of the City respectively. The Barbican Library is the headquarters of the City Lending Libraries service, providing general lending, fine arts books, children's and music libraries, and special loan collections on economics and London studies. The music library has a sound-recording loan service, and books on sports and games have been augmented to form the London Marathon Sports Library. The Children's Library flourishes, although there are only a handful of resident children living in the City; but nursery groups and primary schools near by bring parties for story hours and introductory reading.

Very different is the St Bride Printing Library, opened in 1895, for which the Corporation has been responsible since 1966. For nearly 400 years the western half of the City of London was the centre of English printing and publishing, and the St Bride Foundation Institute was created in 1891 to provide technical education in letterpress printing and lithography as well as recreation for the working population of Fleet Street. It bought the library of William Blades, a City printer and the author of a biography of William Caxton, who introduced printing to England. Blades had collected many books on the history and techniques of his trade and to these were added modern technical books for the Institute's printing school. Among further additions was the library of Talbot Baines Reed, a typefounder by profession, who is remembered as the author of school stories for boys. The printing school soon moved from Bride Lane to other quarters and Fleet Street is no longer full of the old familiar sights and sounds of newsprint and typesetting machinery, but research into the history of books and printing can still be conducted in the area. The St Bride Printing Library has printing types and presses, drawings and manuscripts, as well as one of the largest collections of books and periodicals on its subject.

The City's Records Office houses the most complete and valuable series of municipal archives in the country. Throughout the centuries the Corporation has jealously guarded and preserved records of its own administration, as well as of proceedings in the civic courts dating from the 13th century. The collection includes William I's charter of 1067 and a 1297 copy of the Magna Carta (of which there are only four in existence), as well as many illuminated manuscripts. Corporation members and officers make extensive use of the Records Office, which is also open to students, historians and members of the public interested in the history of the City. A conservation section undertakes skilled restoration work on the archives.

THE MUSEUM OF LONDON

As little as an hour or as long as a day can be spent exploring London's rich history at the Museum of London, which stands at the junction of London Wall and Aldersgate Street. There is no admission charge to this fascinating museum. It has an exciting range of displays, talks, films, and temporary exhibitions on a wide variety of subjects connected with London, often drawing upon the museum's reserve collections. Past exhibitions and displays have included the work of London silversmiths in the 18th century and an exhibition of dolls of all periods. The galleries record Prehistoric, Roman, Medieval, Tudor, Stuart, Georgian, Victorian, and 20th-Century London.

The museum was voted 'Museum of the Year' in the *Good Museum Guide* in 1982 and it is easy to see why. Opened in 1976, it contains the combined and very rich resources of the old Guildhall Museum (founded in 1826) and the London Museum (founded in 1911) which used to be housed in Kensington Palace. At the new Museum of London you can see (to take a random selection) reconstructions of Roman dining rooms, an 18th-century prison cell, Victorian shops (rescued from demolition), the Art Deco lifts which used to be in Selfridges in the 1920s, an early 19th-century Punch and Judy show, a model of the Great Fire of 1666, complete with lighting and sound effects, a medieval shoe found during excavation for a modern City building, and the Lord Mayor's coach, built in 1757. The museum attracts more than half a million visitors each year, including about 90,000 children in organized groups.

This is the way to learn social history! But behind the public face of this lively museum is a serious scientific and educational purpose. The museum has its own archaeological field and research units, the Departments of Urban Archaeology and of Greater London Archaeology. There are specialist collections of books, paintings, prints, drawings, photographs and artefacts open to researchers by appointment. The Education Service provides programmes and activities both for the individual and for organized parties of all ages and abilities, including public lectures and films on London's history, often in connection with special exhibitions. There are workshops in which visitors can meet staff informally and day schools to bring together expert speakers who lecture on specific aspects of London's history. Specialist study days for students give opportunities to examine items from the museum's reserve collection. Teachers' courses and holiday activities for families and children extend the range of services still further.

The Museum of London has a huge costume collection containing clothing made, sold and worn in London. The collection, one of the largest in the world, ranges from Roman times to the present day. There are male and female fashions from Elizabethan times onwards, and it is especially rich in late 19th-century theatre, ballet and music-hall costume. It also includes 20th-century clothes from London shops and from couture houses such as Hardy Amies and Norman Hartnell, together with the work of Continental designers such as Balenciaga, Chanel, Schiaparelli, and Worth. No other museum can boast such a large collection of royal clothing: there are more than 1,000 items,

Queen Victoria's wedding dress, part of the collection of royal clothing in the Museum of London.

A Victorian tobacco shop, reconstructed in the Museum of London.

including Charles I's childhood boots, Princess Charlotte's wedding dress (1816), and many coronation robes. Gloves, hats and underwear complete the collection. Sadly much of this is not on display since the museum does not have the funds to house the collection, but the museum's 'friends of fashion' are helping to raise money for a special extension.

Discovering London's past is a continuous process in which archaeology plays an important part. There is now a very good understanding between the City, developers, construction companies and the Museum of London about the need for 'rescue archaeology'. This is the excavation and recording of sites which takes place in the crucial interval between the demolition of old buildings and the construction of new ones. In the past General Pitt-Rivers, Sir Mortimer Wheeler and Professor W.F. Grimes all made substantial contributions to the archaeology of the City and sporadic and important discoveries were made. The Temple of Mithras in Walbrook, for example, whose existence was suspected as long ago as 1889, was found in 1954 during redevelopment of a bomb-shattered area for Bucklersbury House. It is only since the 1970s, however, that we have begun to have a clear idea of life in Roman and Saxon London. The Museum's Department of Urban Archaeology, founded in 1973, has been at the forefront of these new discoveries.

Outstanding finds in recent years include part of a Roman forum in Leadenhall Street, the Roman quayside at Billingsgate, and a Roman riverside wall at Blackfriars. In 1978, the remains of two late 1st-century courtyard houses were found at Watling Court. They are the first Roman domestic buildings in London for which detailed ground plans exist. In Pudding Lane the remains of early Roman riverside warehouses came to light in 1981, together with part of a merchant's house (or possibly an inn) with a bath-house and latrine. Conclusions can be drawn from many of the objects found. A gold and emerald necklace recovered from a 1st-century Roman timber-lined drain suggests the wealth of Rome and of the many immigrants, who were accustomed to a Mediterranean style of living. Wine jars from Spain and Greece, and fine glass from Italy and Syria have also been excavated: all evidence of the glory that was Rome.

The early Saxons were not city-dwellers. The remains of the Roman city may have been almost deserted for nearly two centuries after the end of the Roman period, until the foundation of the church of St Paul in 604. Then a new London grew up on another site, an international trading port along the north bank of the Thames in the area of the Strand, where archaeology is beginning to reveal traces of occupation stretching from the Aldwych to Whitehall. This merchant town did not survive the Viking raids of the 9th century. When King Alfred won

The excavation of the Roman Temple of Mithras on the east bank of the Walbrook stream in 1954 attracted many visitors. Bucklersbury House now stands on the site.

London back from the Danes in 886 he reoccupied the more easily defended area within the old Roman city walls.

The Saxons built largely in timber. Their houses have left fewer traces in the ground than the earlier Roman stone buildings but recent excavations have produced evidence of the late Saxon town that grew up inside the rebuilt walls of Alfred's time. There is evidence of the manufacture of industrial and domestic goods in metal and bone, and of foreign trade. Queenhithe, Dowgate and Billingsgate are known to have existed as pre-Norman harbours. 'Queenhithe', says Brian Hobley, Chief Urban Archaeologist, 'seems to have served upstream local trade while just downstream, Dowgate, by the first half of the 11th century, served the needs of privileged communities of overseas merchants. Billingsgate, which served both local and overseas trade, first appears in documents of *c.*1000 which represent, in effect, London's earliest harbour regulations, and include the first reference to London Bridge.'

However, it is the Romans who have left the most personal traces of their presence. AUSTALIS DIBUS XIII VAGATUR SIB COTIDIM, wrote a Roman workman, scratching his colloquial Latin on a tile while it was still wet: 'Austalis has been wandering off on his own every day for thirteen days.' SILVI TETRICI EVODES AD ASPRITUDINES, advertised a Roman oculist on a trade work stamp: 'Silvus Tetricus' perfumed ointment for sore eyelids.' QUINTUS, who scratched his name on the wall of the Roman public baths unearthed at Huggins Hill, and the man who wrote GAI SUM PECULIARIS ('I am the property of Gaius') on a pottery vessel, were simply yielding to every schoolboy's desire for immortality.

From letters, tombstones, trademarks and *graffiti* we know the names of seventy or so of the thousands of people (Romans, Britons and immigrants from all parts of the Empire) who inhabited Londinium after the invasion of AD 43. The skulls of citizens massacred in Boudicca's rebellion of AD 61 have been found. It is known that the city was then rebuilt on a grander scale, as the trading capital of the province with a Governor's palace overlooking the river. It is possible to reconstruct a Roman kitchen, with a cooking pot on the open hearth,

A Roman pierced leather shoe of the 1st or 2nd century, found in remarkably good condition in the Walbrook streambed.

A Roman kitchen is one of several rooms reconstructed in the Roman Gallery at the Museum of London.

storage jars and mixing bowls, kitchen knives and ladles, and a quern or handmill for grinding flour for the family's bread. We know what tools Roman carpenters and metalworkers used and what jewellery, hair pins and cosmetics Roman women had on their dressing tables. Apparently people played a game rather like draughts called *ludus latrunculorum* ('game of the bandits'); and one of the stranger finds of recent years was the lower half of a leather bikini (found in a well), which was probably worn by a Roman dancing girl. Most of these discoveries may be seen in the Museum of London.

The museum in Docklands which will reflect a different side of the City's history is expected to open in 1990. It will tell the story of London as the nation's leading port, commercial and industrial centre. Meanwhile a preview of some of its exhibits can be seen at 'W' Warehouse in the Royal Victoria Dock. Among them are reconstructions of the workshops of a rigger, a printer, and a cooper (or barrelmaker). There are also displays of a chandler's wares, cargo handling tools, and a collection of boats. Children may like to try on a diver's helmet and boots, work a foghorn, weigh themselves on a beam scale, operate ropes and pulleys, and practise making knots.

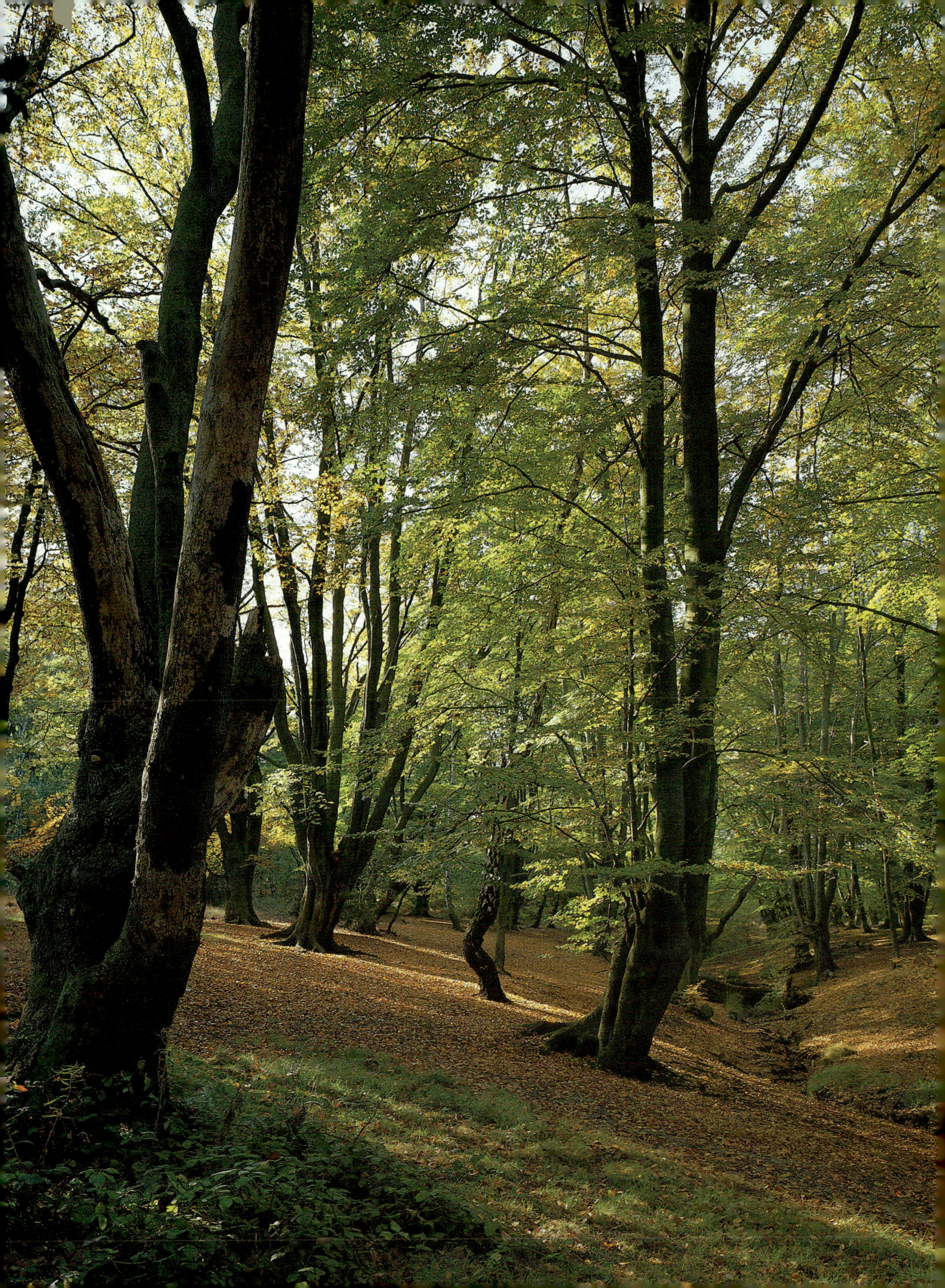

FROM WOODS AND COMMONS TO CITY GARDENS

In 1882 Sir William Sedgewick Saunders, the City's Medical Officer of Health, declared: 'London is already overpopulated. Hence the necessity of providing open spaces for the people; for, unless means are taken to provide parks and recreation grounds for the use of the inhabitants of the Metropolis, the increasing aggregation of human beings in confined spaces will become a source of great danger to public health. Open spaces, therefore, regardless of the cost, should be preserved for the people.'

The Victorian City was a smoky, oppressively cluttered jumble from which people longed to escape. The Corporation fought lawsuits to save land from enclosure, and then acquired Epping Forest, Burnham Beeches and other stretches of unspoilt country outside the City for Londoners to enjoy on high days and holidays. Local people have also benefited by the City's generosity, for these open spaces were (and are) paid for out of City's Cash with no charge on local rates.

The 6,000 acres of Epping Forest are a remnant of the prehistoric forest that once stretched from the Thames to the Wash and across most of East Anglia. It has been suggested that Queen Boudicca fought her last battle with the Romans here, committing suicide with her daughters by eating poisonous berries. In medieval times it was a royal hunting ground and in 1226 Henry III granted the citizens of London the right to hunt in the forest on Easter Monday, a right which the Lord Mayor and Aldermen in particular exercised for many centuries. Henry VIII often hunted there and is said to have been doing so when he heard the gun from the Tower announcing the execution of Anne Boleyn. In the 18th century monarchs paid less attention to hunting, and the forest became the haunt of highwaymen and criminals on the run. The Easter Hunt apparently survived until the latter half of the 19th century but by then it had degenerated into 'a rowdy affair' attended by riff-raff.

The forest was saved for Londoners by the Corporation in 1878. Stretching from Forest Gate for 12 miles into the Essex countryside, it has woods of oak, beech, and birch, and the largest collection of hornbeams in England. There are horse rides, ponds and streams; and herds of black fallow deer have roamed here for centuries. The Epping Forest Conservation Centre, equipped by the Corporation and managed by the Field Studies Council, was opened in 1971. Intended mainly for middle school children, it can also be used by more advanced students, and has laboratories and a resident scientific staff. Queen Elizabeth's Hunting Lodge at Chingford, a three-storey Tudor building from which the monarchs could watch the chase on the ground below, is now the Epping Forest Museum.

Burnham Beeches in Buckinghamshire, some 25 miles west of the City, was acquired by the Corporation in 1880 and has been managed and conserved by it ever since. The wood is the largest collection of old pollarded beech trees in the world, in an area of 504 acres. It seems sad that the trees were originally grown for firewood. The largest tree of all, Druid's Oak, is 9.14 m. (30 ft.) in girth and is believed to be 400 years old. Burnham Beeches is also rich in bird life: over sixty-two

Epping Forest, the largest of the open spaces in and around London owned and maintained by the Corporation of London.

species breed there, and a further twenty species are seasonal visitors.

Place names in the Beeches are associated with personalities who have loved and cared for them: Lord Mayor's Drive; Sir Henry Peek's Drive (Peek was a local philanthropist who bought the enclosed land and resold it to the Corporation); the 'Jenny Lind' tree on whose roots the famous singer used to sit; and 'Mendelssohn's Slope', near Green Drive, where the composer used to rest when visiting England.

Also maintained by the Corporation in their natural state are the commons of Coulsdon, Farthingdown, Kenley and Riddlesdown (in Surrey) and West Wickham Common and Spring Park (in Kent). All are within about 25 miles of the City centre.

Nearer the City is Highgate Wood with its 70 acres of natural woodland. It is mainly a wood of oaks and hornbeams, but many other shrubs and trees grow there, and sixty-nine species of birds have been observed. Both Highgate Wood and Queens Park, Kilburn, a 30-acre public park, were offered to the Corporation by the Ecclesiastical Commissioners in 1885. The money to buy them came from the proceeds of the will of William Ward.

Those with a taste for unusual graveyards should visit Bunhill Fields, in City Road. It is a place of pilgrimage for Nonconformists, particularly Quakers, many of whom are buried here. There are a number of interesting Latin epitaphs, which tend to be long and

A humorous depiction of the Easter Hunt in Epping Forest, from The Illustrated London News, *1843. The quarry is a stag.*

aggressively anti-Papist. In 1665 the Corporation made a new churchyard here for victims of the Plague, but it was never used for this purpose. As an ordinary cemetery it was soon needed by Nonconformists whose meeting houses seldom had any space for burial grounds. Bunhill Fields was bombed in the Second World War and the northern part was subsequently laid out as a garden. Among famous people buried here are John Bunyan, Daniel Defoe, William Blake, and several members of the Cromwell family.

In the City itself there are 192 open spaces which are cared for by the Corporation. These can be seen by climbing to the top of the Monument or taking the lift to the twenty-fourth floor of the Stock Exchange. There are numerous patches of green space, and carefully placed trees; window-boxes ablaze with flowers, lest the eye should tire of stone and concrete; and the unexpected small gardens where City workers can eat their lunch-time sandwiches. Many of these are very small, no more than a tree and a couple of seats. Some, like St Dunstan in the East, are made from disused churchyards or ruined churches. The largest of all is in Finsbury Circus, an oval garden surrounded by office buildings near Moorgate Underground station. Band concerts are given here in the summer and there is even a public bowling green.

Many of these open spaces were created by the Corporation during

Postman's Park, next to St Botolph's, Aldersgate, is one of many small City gardens. It was formerly the churchyard of St Botolph's and of two other nearby churches.

A window-box brightens a cash dispenser in the City.

the replanning of the City after the widespread destruction caused by the Second World War. They are now the responsibility of the Corporation's Superintendent of Parks and Gardens. 'City gardening creates special problems,' says the Superintendent. 'Petrol fumes, poor soil, pigeons and wind all take their toll. Nearly 250,000 spring and summer bedding plants are raised at the Corporation's nursery at West Ham, and we plant tens of thousands of bulbs every year.' Many City companies have responded to a 'Flowers in the City' campaign by providing their own window-boxes.

Playing bowls on the green in the gardens at the centre of Finsbury Circus.

CUSTOMS AND TRADITIONS

Despite the many changes that have taken place in the City, the past is still remembered in the celebration of old traditions and customs. The Lord Mayor's Show is the most spectacular of these, but there are many other interesting annual ceremonies.

A tradition dating back to the 10th century can be observed at certain livery company banquets at which guests drink from a huge loving cup. As the cup is passed round, each guest protects his neighbour by standing back to back with him. The tradition is a reminder of the murder in AD 978 of King Edward the Martyr, who was stabbed in the back, apparently on the orders of his mother-in-law Elfrida, while drinking a cup of wine.

The Clothworkers' Company have a drinking tradition of their own. After dinner waiters ask each guest, 'Do you dine, Sir (or Madam), with Alderman or with Lady Cooper?' This means, 'Would you prefer to drink brandy or gin?' and is a custom which originated in the 17th century when Alderman Cooper, having dined well but unwisely, dropped dead on his return home. His wife, Lady Cooper, accused the Clothworkers of plying her husband with too much brandy. When she herself died, she left money in her will to provide gin for the Company's guests as a more suitable alternative to brandy.

The Trial of the Pyx is a ceremony, probably of Saxon or even Roman origin, which takes place at the Goldsmiths' Hall every February or March. It is conducted by the Queen's Remembrancer and a jury drawn from the Royal Mint and the Goldsmiths' Company. Their task is to test samples of newly minted coins of the realm to ensure that they are of the proper weight and metallic composition. The samples are placed in the Pyx (or Mint Box). The jury's verdicts are delivered to the Queen's Remembrancer in May, in the presence of the Chancellor of the Exchequer, who is Master of the Mint.

Schoolchildren are involved in several of the City's ceremonies, since many charitable schools were founded by City benefactors. On or near 20 February each year a service is held at St Botolph's, Aldgate in memory of Sir John Cass, the City Sheriff who founded the school named after him, in 1709. The service is attended by pupils wearing red feather quills in their hats and lapels. Sir John died of a haemorrhage while drawing up his will for the benefit of the Foundation, and the red quills represent his bloodstained pen.

Part of the choir of Christ's Hospital (the 'Bluecoat School') attend the Spital Sermon, preached on the second Thursday after Easter at St Lawrence Jewry. The sermon is associated with the Priory or Hospital of St Mary Spital, near the site of Spitalfields Market, which was founded by Walter and Rose Brune in 1197 for the care of the poor and sick. Christ's Hospital was founded in 1552 in Newgate Street as a charitable foundation and it soon became traditional for the boys to attend the sermon preached from an open-air pulpit called the Spital Cross. The Hospital of St Mary Spital was closed for lack of money in 1838 but the sermon continues, attended by the Lord Mayor, Aldermen and other City dignitaries who walk in procession to the church from Guildhall. Although Christ's Hospital moved to Horsham in Sussex in 1902, a small group of choir members return to London each year to attend the sermon.

A service of dedication and thanksgiving for the foundation of Bridewell is held at St Bride's, Fleet Street, on the second Tuesday in March. Bridewell was a royal palace built for Henry VIII on the banks of the Fleet River, and was given to the City by Edward VI as a refuge for vagrants and homeless children and, partly, as a prison. The foundation service is attended by the Lord Mayor and Sheriffs, and by the children of King Edward VI School, Witley, Surrey.

Signor Pasquale Favale was a romantic Italian merchant who left money in 1880 to provide marriage dowries for three 'poor honest' young women between the ages of 18 and 25 who were either born in the City or had lived there for seven years. He said in his will that he had been induced to make the bequest by the fact that his wife was a native of London, and he had passed many years of his life in that City. The money is distributed in April.

Another charitable distribution, made every Good Friday after the 11 a.m. service, is the presentation of hot cross buns and coins to 'poor widows' at St Bartholomew-the-Great, Smithfield. The gifts come from the Butterworth Charity, and are laid out on tombstones outside the west door of the church.

On or near 5 April a service is held at St Andrew Undershaft, Leadenhall Street, in commemoration of John Stow, the 16th-century historian and antiquary to whom we owe so much of our knowledge of the City in early times. During the service the Lord Mayor puts a new quill pen into the hand of Stow's statue. The old quill is presented, together with a prize, for the best essay on London by a pupil of a London school.

Samuel Pepys, another of London's famous writers, is also remembered annually, at a service on or near 26 May at St Olave's, Hart

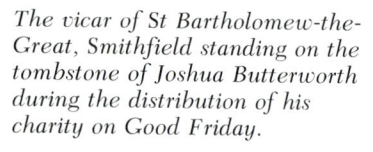

The vicar of St Bartholomew-the-Great, Smithfield standing on the tombstone of Joshua Butterworth during the distribution of his charity on Good Friday.

The monument to John Stow, author of the Survey of London, *was erected in St Andrew Undershaft in 1905 (the tercentenary of his death) by the Merchant Taylors' Company of which he was a member.*

Street. Both Pepys and his wife are buried there. The service is attended by the Lord Mayor and Sheriffs, as well as by the Master and Wardens of the Clothworkers' Company, of which Pepys was a member.

In a City which has been governing itself for over a thousand years it should not be a surprise that there are still Aleconners, four freemen of the City with an annual expenses allowance of £10 each. They are elected on Midsummer Day (21 June) and their duty, defined in medieval times, is to taste the brewers' wares to ensure that they are 'as good ales, or better' than they were 'wont to brew'.

Also at Midsummer, members of Tower ward and parishioners of All Hallows by the Tower present a single red rose to the Lord Mayor (and a whole bouquet to the Lady Mayoress) at the Mansion House. The origin of this custom dates back to 1381, when the Lord Mayor imposed a quit rent on Constance, wife of Sir Robert Knollys, who had built a bridge from her house in Seething Lane to a building across the street. She had not asked permission to do this but since her husband was abroad, fighting the French, the Lord Mayor took a lenient view and gallantly demanded an annual rose from her garden. The custom seems to have lapsed during the 17th century but was revived in 1924 and has continued ever since.

In July, the Vintners' Company walk in procession to their church, St James's, Garlickhythe on Garlick Hill from their Hall in Upper Thames Street, following the annual election of their officials. A wine porter, wearing a white smock and top hat, goes before the procession sweeping the road clear with a besom broom. This is a reminder of the days when the streets were full of mire and filth.

Swan Upping is one of two river customs that take place in July. In the third week of the month all the cygnets between London Bridge and Henley are rounded up and 'upped' or given marks of ownership. The Thames swans belong either to the Queen, who owns 500, or to one of two City companies, the Vintners or Dyers. The Vintners' swans are marked with two nicks on their upper beaks, the Dyers' birds have one nick and the Queen's none at all. The team of eighteen watermen are led by John Turk of Cookham, the Royal Swan Keeper, whose family have been Thames watermen since 1750. There have been Royal Swan Keepers since about 1300. A Swan Feast is held periodically when the Master of the Vintners' Company is presented with roast cygnets 'to the music of woodwind instruments'.

Doggett's Coat and Badge Race is the other July river event. The oldest boat race in England, it is rowed with sculls for 5 miles between London Bridge and Cadogan Pier, Chelsea by six members of the Watermen's Company who have just completed their apprenticeship. The race was founded by Thomas Doggett, an Irish comedian, who wished to express his gratitude to London watermen, who were much in demand when London Bridge was the only bridge across the Thames. He was also a fervent royalist and in 1715 founded the race for watermen to compete for 'the Livery and Badge provided yearly under the Will of the late Mr Thos. Doggett in commemoration of the happy Accession of His Majesty George the First to the Throne of Great Britain in 1714.' The original prize was a scarlet skirted coat with a large silver arm-badge bearing the horse of Hanover.

On St Matthew's Day (21 September) a service is held at St Sepulchre's, Holborn, attended by the Lord Mayor, Sheriffs and Aldermen, together with boys and girls from Christ's Hospital, including the full choir. After the service the school's marching band

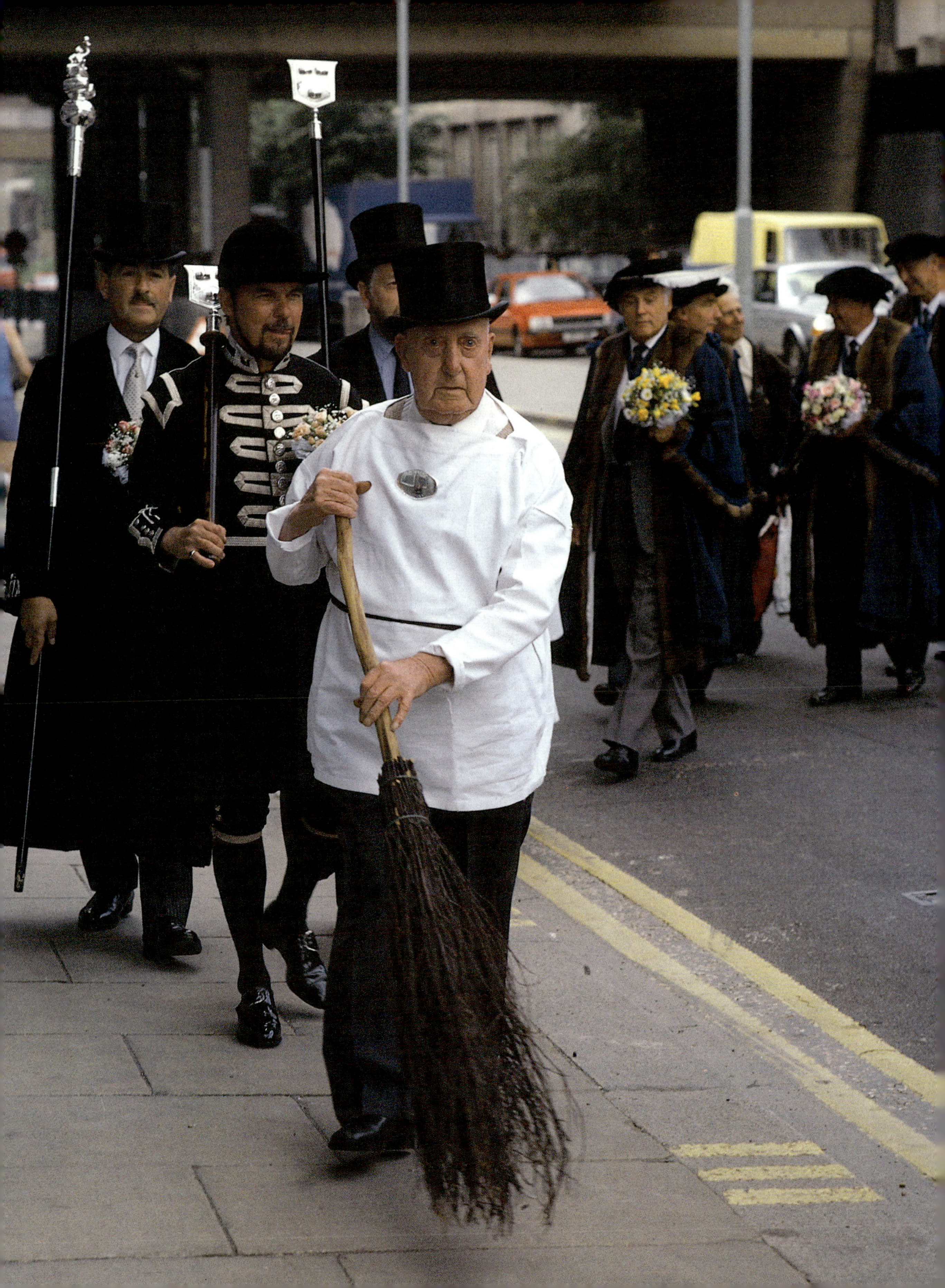

right: *Swan uppers at Boulter's Lock during the annual four-day progress along the Thames when new cygnets are counted and 'upped'.*

left: *A wine porter sweeps the road in front of the Vintners' Company procession, which is led by the Bargemaster, Beadle and Clerk, followed by the new Master, the Wardens and Court of Assistants.*

leads the procession of nearly 400 pupils to Guildhall, where they are entertained to lunch by the Lord Mayor, who also gives them each a small gift.

The day after Michaelmas, or as near to it as possible, a strange rite takes place at the Law Courts in the Strand. The Comptroller and City Solicitor pays the Queen's Remembrancer token rents for two holdings, the Moors in Shropshire and the Forge at St Clement Danes in the Strand. Known as the Quit Rents ceremony, it dates back at least to the 13th century. For the Moors, whose location is uncertain, the rent paid is two knives, one sharp enough to 'cut a hazel stick with one blow', and the other so weak that it would 'bend in new cheese'. For a time these knives were replaced by a billhook (blunt) and a hatchet (sharp). The Forge property is paid for by six horseshoes and sixty-one nails. This apparently originated from jousting tournaments held on

75

Past winners of the annual Doggett's Coat and Badge sculling race wearing the magnificent uniform which is the prize.

adjoining land. New knives are made every year, but the horseshoes and nails are always the same.

The month of November is so dominated by the ceremonies surrounding the installation of the new Lord Mayor, including the 'Silent Change', the Lord Mayor's Show and the Banquet, that there is no room left for any minor ceremonies.

Every year early in December the Lord Mayor makes a tour of Smithfield Market and is presented with a boar's head on a silver platter by the Worshipful Company of Butchers. This ceremony is a fairly recent revival of a medieval tradition, which began when the butchers were granted a piece of land near the Fleet River on which to

The pupils of Christ's Hospital assemble outside Guildhall following the St Matthew's Day service at St Sepulchre's, Holborn.

wash their meat. The old practice of leaving the entrails of slaughtered beasts near the Greyfriars Monastery was understandably not welcomed by the monks. In gratitude the butchers undertook to maintain a wharf in the area, and to make the annual presentation of the boar's head.

A grand Christmas Pudding is also presented to the Lord Mayor in December by the Australian High Commissioner. This is donated to charity, and the year is rounded off with a children's party held at the Mansion House.

The ancient Quit Rents ceremony, illustrated in The Graphic, *1906.*

77

EXPLORING THE CITY'S CHURCHES

The late Poet Laureate, Sir John Betjeman, lived for some years in Cloth Fair, Smithfield. A great lover of the City, he used to conduct parties of visitors round its streets, explaining everything they saw, particularly its churches. He taught them to observe architectural features and monuments and to re-create history from

A 17th-century view of London Bridge and the City before most of the spires silhouetted against the sky were destroyed in the Great Fire.

them, without resorting slavishly to guide books. This was his great hobby and he called it 'church-crawling'.

There were 107 parish churches in the City before 1666, but eighty-six were lost in the Great Fire. Sir Christopher Wren ('that miracle' as his friend John Evelyn called him), who only became an architect in his thirties after successful careers as a mathematician, artist and astronomer, rebuilt fifty-one of them. In 1939 there were still forty-seven Anglican churches in the Square Mile. Many suffered badly in the air-raids of 1940–1, although twenty-three of Wren's churches survived. Seven were never rebuilt but the towers of six remain. One church, St Mary Aldermanbury, was taken down stone by stone and re-erected at Fulton, Missouri, to commemorate Sir Winston Churchill's

opposite: St Paul's Cathedral from the south, showing the full splendour of Wren's dome topped by its baroque stone lantern and gold ball and cross.

famous speech in which he spoke of the 'iron curtain' dividing Europe.

Today there are twenty-three parish churches and fifteen guild churches in the City. The latter do not hold regular services but are devoted to special purposes. Thus St Lawrence Jewry next Guildhall is the Corporation of London's civic church, and St Ethelburga-the-Virgin within Bishopsgate is associated with healing. Some churches have lunch-time recitals and concerts.

The greatest church of all is, of course, St Paul's Cathedral, scene of royal weddings, state funerals and splendid music from its famous choir. It is believed that a Roman temple of Diana was the first ecclesiastical building on this site, and that the first Christian church was founded here in 604 by Ethelbert, King of Kent, who dedicated it to St Paul. Burnt down (it was probably built of wood), it was replaced in the 7th century by a stone building which was destroyed by Vikings in 961. A third Saxon cathedral was gutted by fire in 1087, to be replaced by the huge cathedral that Pepys saw on fire in 1666. This had

The glorious interior of St Paul's has been the setting for a long line of national celebrations, including the wedding of the Prince of Wales and Lady Diana Spencer on 29 July, 1981.

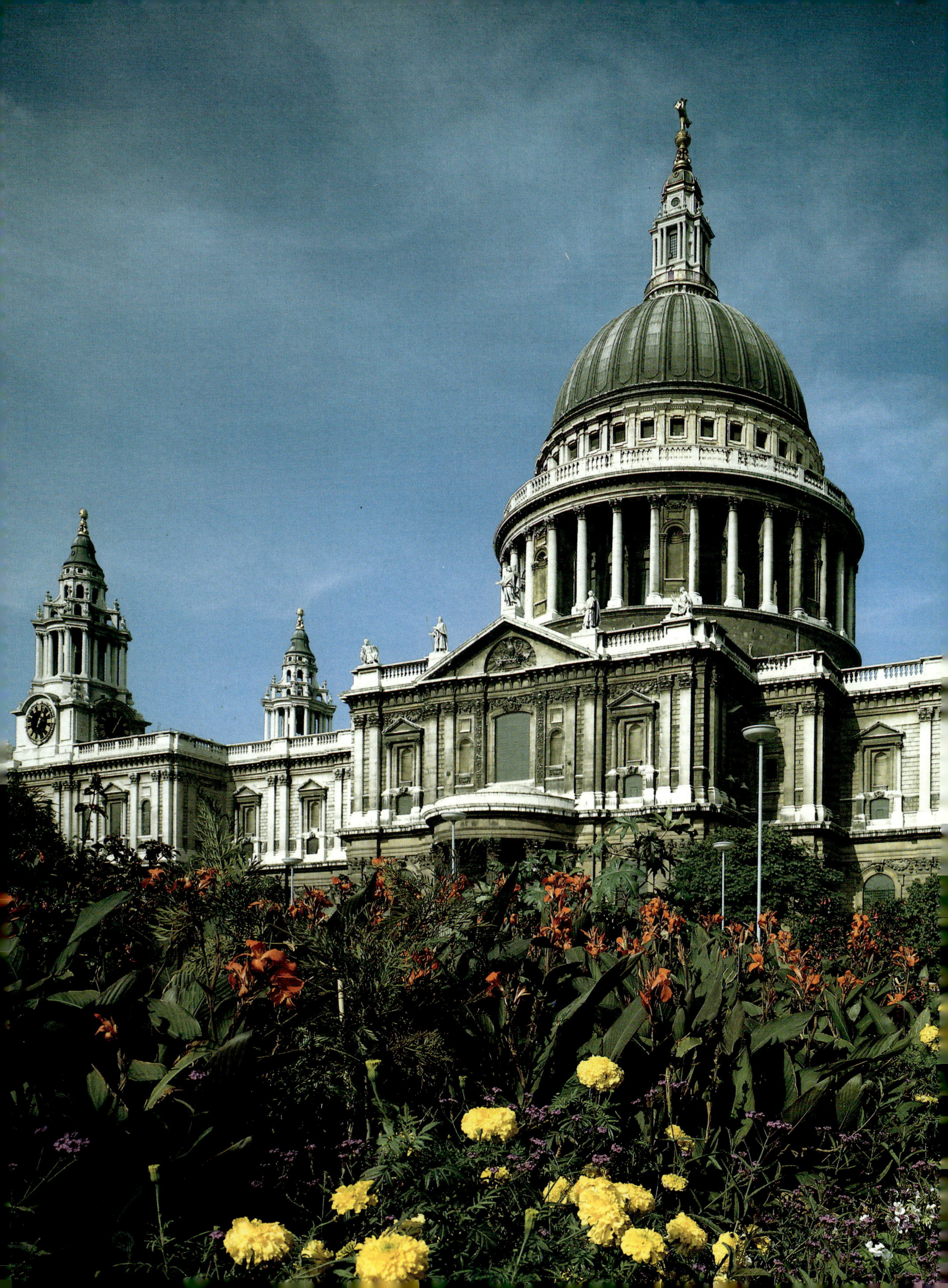

Sir Christopher Wren is renowned for the quality and variety of his church spires, some of which are shown here.

right: *Christ Church, Newgate Street*

below: *St Vedast-alias-Foster*

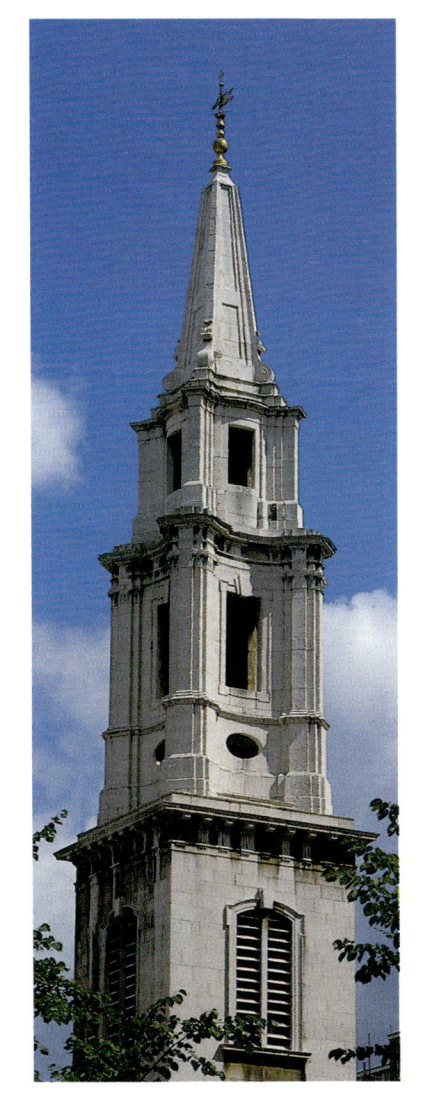

been in a sad state after the Civil War, when Cromwell's soldiers had smashed windows and monuments and used the nave as a cavalry barracks.

Wren made three designs for the new cathedral. The second, known as the Great Model, was his own favourite and he is said to have wept when it was rejected. The all-important decision was to break away from Gothic, which Wren disliked, and have a classical dome like that of St Peter's in Rome instead of a tall steeple. He was a many-talented Renaissance man *par excellence* and one of the very few cathedral architects to have seen his building completed in his lifetime. Begun in 1675, it was finished in 1711, when he was 79 (and still had more than a decade to live).

The crypt, where Nelson, Wellington, Sir Arthur Sullivan and Wren himself are buried, the Thornhill frescos of the life of St Paul, and the Whispering Gallery (sounds can be heard on the opposite side of the Gallery 32.6 m. (107 ft.) away, so perfect are the acoustics) are but a small part of the cathedral's memorable features. St Paul's, defended by fire-fighters during the Blitz on London, was a symbol of survival during World War II; and its gratitude to its American ally is expressed in the American Chapel behind the High Altar.

St Paul's has a great choral tradition, based on eight centuries of sung services. The great leap forward in musical excellence was achieved by John Stainer, organist from 1872, who shaped the famous Choir School as we know it today and began the annual performances, with orchestra, of Bach's Passion music in Holy Week and Handel's *Messiah* in Advent. Visitors may hear it at sung eucharist at 11 a.m. in the cathedral on summer Sundays. The choir has taken part in many royal occasions, notably the wedding of the Prince and Princess of Wales in 1981.

In the City you are seldom more than a street away from a church. The City's oldest surviving church is St Bartholomew-the-Great, Smithfield, originally part of an Augustinian priory founded in 1123 by Rahere who was one of Henry I's courtiers, and may have been his court jester. It is said that he founded the church in gratitude to St

above: *St James's, Garlickhythe*

right: *St Bride's, Fleet Street*

below: *St Michael Paternoster Royal*

St Mary-le-Bow, one of Wren's most magnificent churches, completed in 1680.

opposite: St Lawrence Jewry next Guildhall, rebuilt by Wren after the Great Fire, is now the church of the Corporation of London. The new Guildhall offices of the Corporation are on the left.

Bartholomew for saving him from a monster or, perhaps, from malaria while he was on a pilgrimage to Rome. The church and monastic buildings have been put to some strange uses. The crypt was once a coal and wine cellar. The Lady Chapel has been a private house and a printing office (where Benjamin Franklin learnt his trade in 1725). The north transept once accommodated a blacksmith's forge. Rahere, whose 16th-century tomb is north of the sanctuary, also founded St Bartholomew's, London's oldest hospital. Smithfield Market is very close, and the Butchers' Company hold their annual service in the church.

A true Cockney is someone born within the sound of Bow Bells, provided by a City mercer in 1472 to be rung as a curfew every night at nine o'clock. They were destroyed by the bombing of St Mary-le-Bow, Cheapside, in 1941. The BBC, which had used them as a time-signal before the war, fortunately had a recording of the bells, and this was broadcast to Occupied Europe as a symbol of defiance and survival. A church certainly stood here before 1090, but was burnt down in the Great Fire and rebuilt with a magnificent 'wedding cake' steeple

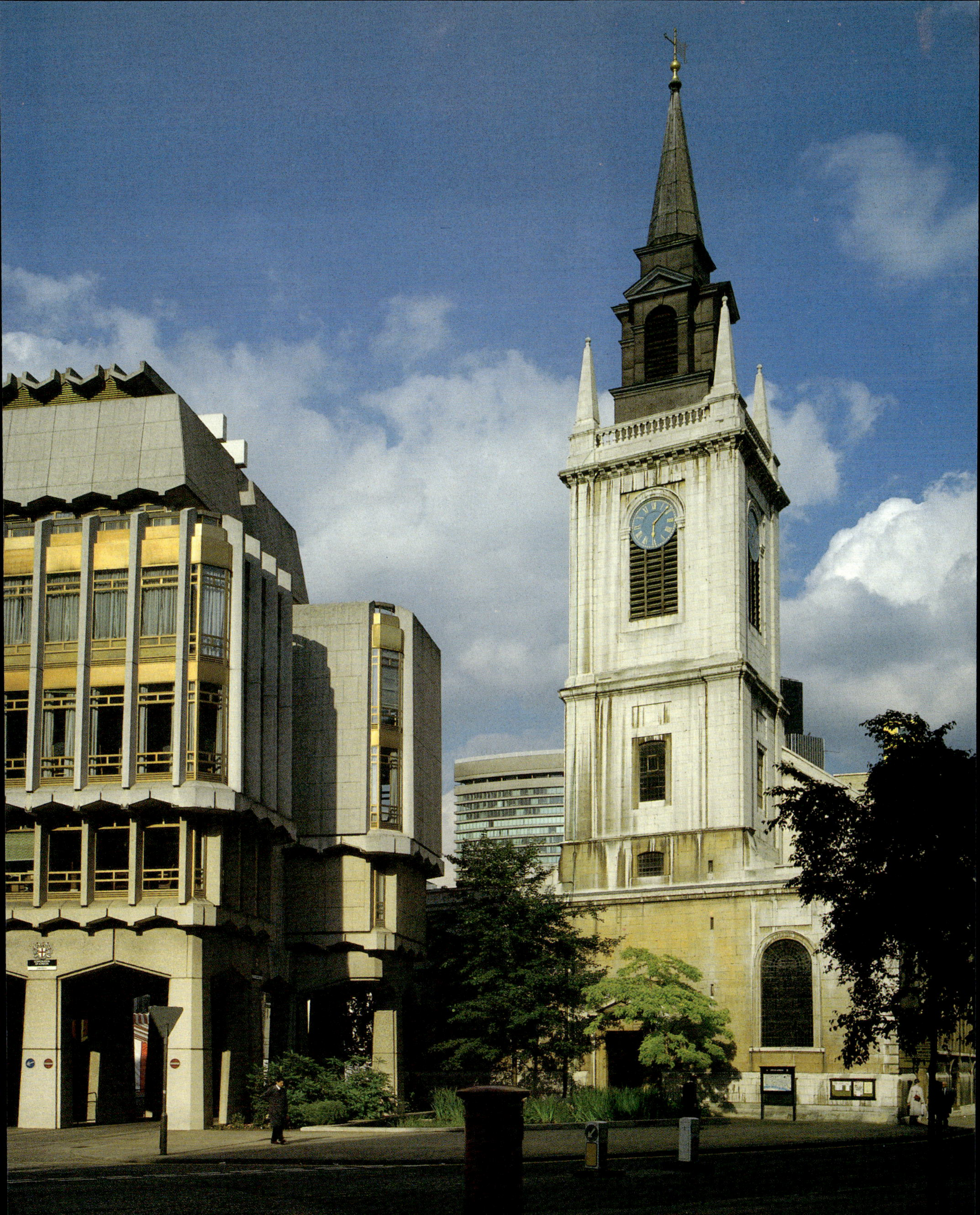

The interior of St Mary at Hill, one of the earliest of Wren's churches to be completed (1677). It has been carefully and sensitively restored.

opposite: St Benet's, Paul's Wharf, a charming example of Wren's work.

(66 m./217 ft. high) by Wren in 1670. The only remains of the old church are the Norman arches in the crypt, which may have given the church the name 'le-Bow'. The old churchyard is now a piazza, with a statue of Captain John Smith, whose life was saved by the Red Indian princess Pocohontas in Virginia in 1608. A new peal of bells was installed in 1961, and first rung by Prince Philip.

The City's smallest church is St Ethelburga-the-Virgin within Bishopsgate. Ethelburga was the daughter of Offa, King of Mercia, and her church is believed to date from the 13th century. Before 1933 it had to be entered by a sort of tunnel between 16th-century houses which were pulled down to widen the pavement. The humble church thus revealed gives us an idea of what many City churches must have looked like before 1666, for the Great Fire did not reach this far. It is a jumble of styles. There is a 17th-century weathercock, a square 18th-century belfry, and a 15th-century window above a 14th-century door. The 17th-century east window bears the arms of the City and three livery companies, Mercers, Saddlers and Vintners; and three windows of 1928 show Henry Hudson and the men who took Communion here before sailing in search of the North-West Passage in 1607.

Another 'wedding cake' steeple is that of St Bride's, Fleet Street; indeed, it may be because of it (and it is probably Wren's best, ascending in five beautifully proportioned tiers) that wedding cakes are made as they are. An older church was destroyed in the Great Fire. Its antiquity was only discovered in 1940 after an air-raid, when Professor Grimes examined the crypt and found the remains of a Roman house and a 6th-century Christian church dedicated to St Bridget of Kildare. In the Norman church that succeeded it, Wynkyn

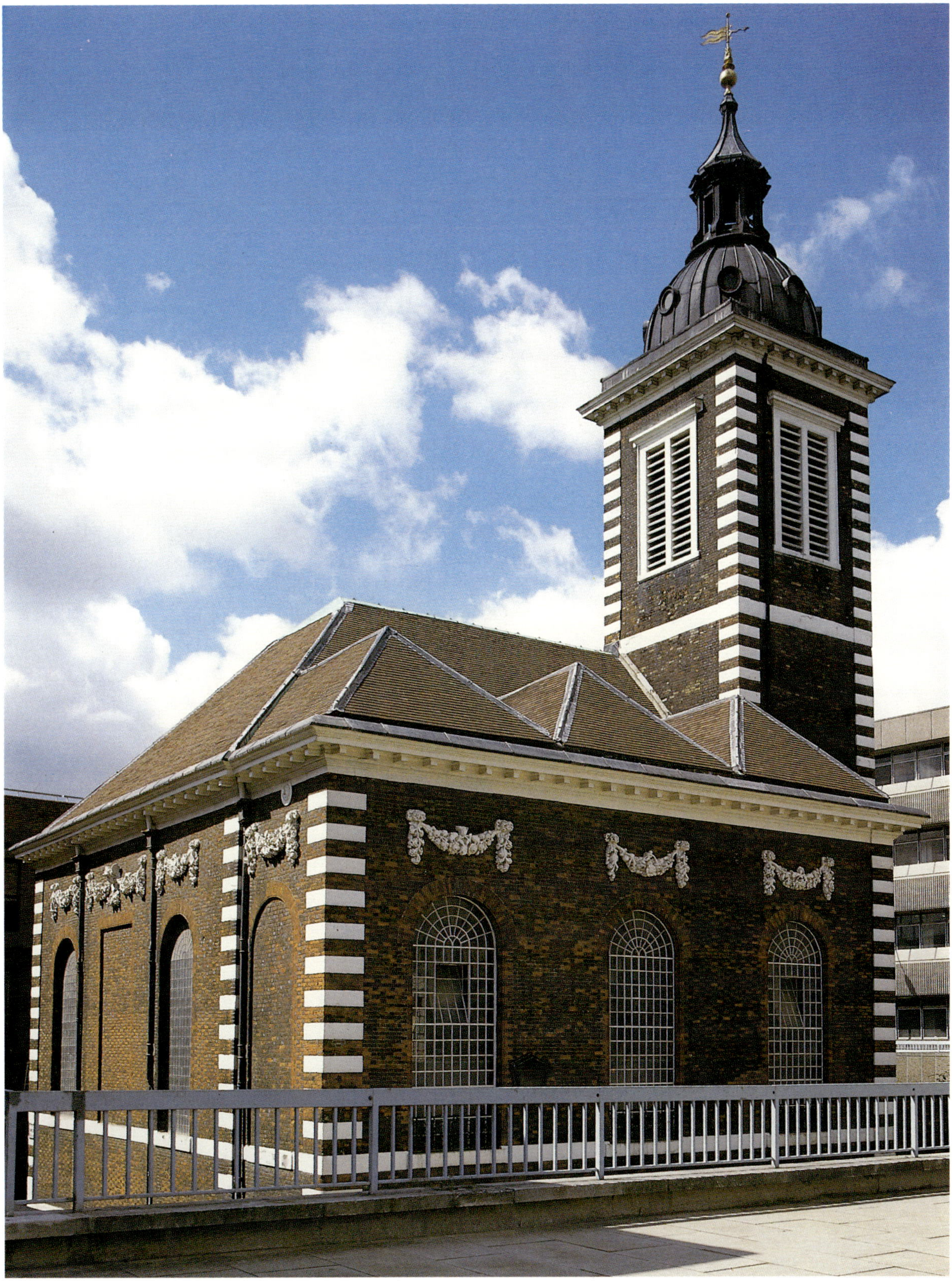

de Worde, who brought the printing press to Fleet Street, was buried; the parents of Virginia Dare, the first English child born in America, worshipped; and the parents of Edward Winslow, one of the Pilgrim Fathers, were married. There Samuel Pepys and his eight brothers and sisters were baptized, and his brother Tom was buried. Inside, the 'Cathedral of Fleet Street' has pews named after great newspapers and journalists, many of whom contributed to its rebuilding after the war. The interior is cheerful and proportioned as only Wren knew how, but it is the steeple that one remembers. It has been called a 'madrigal in stone'.

Also in Fleet Street is the Temple Church, one of the five round churches in England, and the only one in London. The nave is circular (called the 'Round') and the chancel is the 'Oblong'. The Round may have been modelled on the Holy Sepulchre in Jerusalem, or the Dome of the Rock, although opinions on this differ. The church was built in the 12th century by the Knights Templar who were formed to protect pilgrims to the Holy Land, but much of what you see today is loving restoration, for the church was gutted in the air-raids of 1940–1. However, 12th-century effigies of the Templars can still be seen, although badly damaged. Lawyers of the Middle Temple sit in the southern part of the Choir and those of the Inner Temple in the north; their respective arms are displayed on the two main windows. The central window was presented by the Glaziers' Company after the post-war restoration.

In Lower Thames Street is St Magnus the Martyr. Readers of T.S. Eliot's *The Waste Land* will remember his description of the interior: 'inexplicable splendour of Ionian white and gold'. There was a church here at the end of old London Bridge as long ago as 1066, and Miles Coverdale, translator of the New Testament, was its vicar for two years, from 1564–6. He is buried here, as is William Yevele, grandest of medieval architects, who died in 1400. He designed part of Westminster Hall. This is another church 'rebuilt by Wren', who was working on some fifty other churches while St Paul's was rising. When Billingsgate was next door, St Magnus' was never quite free from the smell of fish. Now it smells pleasantly of incense.

The Romans built their first settlement on the banks of a stream called the Walbrook, which was their main water supply. Now it survives in a deep pipe out of sight, and as the name of a street alongside the Mansion House in which you will find St Stephen's, Walbrook. Wren used it to try out certain ideas for St Paul's Cathedral, combining what we now call baroque with English tradition and including a dome and Corinthian columns, amid much other rich interior decoration, some of it the gift of the Grocers' Company. Sir John Vanbrugh, architect of Blenheim Palace, is buried here. There has been much controversy about the new stone altar, carved by Henry Moore. The Rector, the Revd Chad Varah, founded the Samaritans here in 1953: they now have 200 branches where volunteers offer advice and comfort to those who telephone in despair.

For Lutherans, or speakers of Estonian and Latvian, there is the church of St Anne and St Agnes, Gresham Street. The Spanish and Portuguese Synagogue in Bevis Marks, where the Disraeli family worshipped, was built in 1701 by a Quaker, Joseph Avis. There is a modern Dutch church among the stockbrokers in Old Broad Street, while St Benet's, in Upper Thames Street, a cheerful, pretty Wren church, is the London church of the Welsh Episcopalians. These are only a small selection of the extraordinary range of City churches.

TAKING TIME OUT

Does anyone working or living in this twenty-four-hour City have time for leisure? Surprisingly, some do, and even the most hard-working can still fit in a quick work-out or swim at one of the City clubs or sports centres. During the summer months the little gardens and open spaces are suddenly filled with people enjoying a sandwich in the lunch hour and business chatter overflows into the alleyways and streets as office-workers relax and enjoy a drink with colleagues in the sun.

There is lunch-time entertainment too. Throughout the year concerts, poetry readings, and lectures take place in many of the City churches, whose cool charm is a welcome relief from the bustle and noise of a busy office or street. A programme of open-air band concerts is organized by the Corporation at Finsbury Circus, Tower Hill, Paternoster Square and on the steps of St Paul's Cathedral, with music for all tastes from jazz to regimental. Both the Barbican Centre and the Museum of London mount a range of exhibitions, and one of the largest lending libraries in London is also to be found in the Barbican.

Twenty years ago there were very few shopping facilities in the area and the City's high rateable values still prevent the major department stores moving into the Square Mile, but there are now numerous smaller shops selling clothes, books and records, jewellery, and even hardware, and the tiny bakeries and top-quality sandwich bars thrive, feeding bankers, brokers, market makers and other City workers.

Restaurants are one of the City's specialities with every kind of cuisine available on the doorstep – traditional English, French, Italian, Chinese, and Japanese, as well as fish restaurants and others which are exclusively vegetarian. The trend of business entertaining has changed since deregulation in October 1986. Many people are working longer hours, trading with the international markets in Tokyo and New York whose working hours overlap those of London at the opening and close of trading. After an early morning breakfast meeting the day may be broken only by a working lunch and end with a briefing meeting late at night.

The City has its own special charm with medieval buildings standing alongside the most up-to-date architecture. To think of the City as a

Office workers relax during the lunch hour outside one of the City's many attractive pubs and wine bars.

A regimental band concert on the steps of St Paul's Cathedral.

village is not so far from the truth. There is even a flower show held in Guildhall which creates a lively garden fête atmosphere, with prizes for flowers, vegetables and handicrafts. Entries come from City business people as well as from horticulturalists throughout the country.

The unique character of the City lies in the unusual balance it strikes between old and new, commerce and people. Within an area of only one square mile a premier financial centre thrives alongside the buildings and traditions of the historic guilds from which it evolved. The Corporation of London, the democratically elected local authority for this London borough, provides the services and management which ensure the happy balance between the needs of the residential community and the fluctuating daily working population. In the Guildhall, at the heart of the City, members of the Court of Common Council debate issues and make decisions which ensure the continued success of the City far into the next century.

INDEX

Numbers in *italic* refer to illustrations

Abbado, Claudio 51
Abbott, Dr Edwin 57
Admiral of the Port of London 16
Aldermanbury 55
Aldermen 13, 16, 46, 67
Aldwych 63
Aldwych Theatre 51
Alfred, King, 7, 63, 64
All Hallows 73
Amies, Hardy 61
Amis, Kingsley 57
Animal Quarantine Station 41, *41*
archaeology 61, 62, 63
Archbishop of Canterbury 19
Arne, Thomas 55
Ashcroft, Dame Peggy 51
Ashtead Park 57
Askew, Anne 13
Asquith, H. H. 57
Astaire, Fred 56
Avis, Joseph 88

Baltic Exchange 34, *34*
Bamme, Adam 20
Banister, John 54–5
banking 32–3
Bank of England 11, 32–3
Barbican Library 60, 89
Barbican Centre *26*, 48–52, *48, 52*, 55, 89
 concert hall 50, *50*
Barbican Committee 50
Barclays Bank 33
Barclays de Zoete Wedd 29
Barry, Sir John Wolfe 38
Bartholomew Fair 42
Basinghall Street 58, 60
Batchelor, Marjorie 36
Becket, St Thomas à 36
Beckford, William 15, 21
Beecham, Sir Thomas 51
Belfast, HMS 37
Besch, Anthony 50
Betjeman, Sir John 78
Billingsgate Market 30, 43–4
 porters *44*
 bell 43
Bishopsgate 46
Bishopsgate Library 60
Blackfriars 63
Blackfriars Bridge 25, 36
Black Death 9
Blackman, Honor 56
Blades, William 60
Blake, William 69
Bloodworth, Sir Thomas 22
Bloom, Claire 56
'Bluecoat School' 71
Boudicca, Queen 6, 64, 67
Bow Bells 20, 84
Bread Street 8
Brearley, Mike 57
Bridewell 72
Bridge House Estates 24, 36
bridges 35–8, *36, 37, 38*
Britannia 7, 15, 18
Broadgate 30
brokers 33, 34
Brook, Peter 51
Brown, John 36
Bucklersbury House 63, *63*
bullion market 34
Bunhill Fields 52, 68, 69
Bunyan, John 69
Butterworth Charity 72

Butterworth, Joshua, tombstone of *72*
Burnham Beeches 67
Bury, William 58
Bytheway, Joanne 36

Cade, Jack 37
Caesar, Julius 6
Campbell, Mrs Patrick 56
Canute 7
Carlyle, Thomas 54
Carmelite Street 57
Carpenter, John 56
Cass, Sir John 71
Central Criminal Court 26, 46–7
Chamberlain of London 26, 27
Chancellor of the Exchequer 71
Chancellor, Richard 9
Charles II 37, 55
Chief Magistrate of the City 16
Chigwell, Hamo de 20
Christ Church *82*
Christ's Hospital 71, 73, 77
churches 78–88
Churchill, Sir Winston 14, 79
City Business Library 60
City Marshal 20, 46
City of London
 administration 23–30
 commercial growth 8
 environmental quality 29
 financial centre 31–4, 89
 government 9
 rates 24
 rebuilding 11
City of London Freemen's School 57, *57*
City of London Police 45–6
City of London School 30, 56, 57
City of London School for Girls 57
City's Cash 24, 44, 50, 56, 67
Civil War 9, 17, 80
clearing banks 33
Clock Museum, Guildhall 59, *60*
Cloth Fair 78
Cohen, Mr Deputy Stanley 41
Colet, Dean 8
commodities markets 34
Common Cryer and Serjeant-at-Arms 20, 24, 46
Common Hall 12, 16, *16*
Common Serjeant 28, 46
Comptroller and City Solicitor 26, 27, 75
conservation areas 29
Conservatory, Barbican Centre 51, *52*
Cooper, Alderman and Lady 71
Copley, John 22
Corporation of London 15, 23–30, 90
 legal services 28
 motto of 24
 officers of 25–8
 offices 12, *84*
Coulsdon Common 68
Court of Aldermen 16, 17, 20, 23
Court of Common Council 12, 16, 23–4, 23, 90
Coverdale, Miles 88
Coward, Noel 56
Cranmer, Archbishop 13
Crippen, Dr 46
Cripplegate 6
Cromwell, Oliver 52
Crosby, Brass 22
Crystal Palace 42
Curtis, William 22

Custom House *40*
customs 71–7

Dance, George, the Elder 20
Danes 7, 64
Dare, Virginia 88
Defoe, Daniel 69
Docklands 43, 65, 89
Doggett's Coat and Badge race 73, *76*
Doggett, Thomas 73
Donaldson, Dame Mary 19
Dowgate 64
Druid's Oak 67
Dudley, Lord Guildford 14

Easter Hunt, Epping Forest 67, *68*
East India Company 9
Edward IV 72
Edward VI 14
Edward VII 38
Edward the Confessor 7, 13, 14
Edward the Martyr 71
Egyptian Hall, Mansion House 20, *21*
Elfrida 71
Elizabeth I 9
Embankment 35
Epping Forest 67, *67*
 Conservation Centre 67
 Museum 67
Ethelbert of Kent 80
Ethelburga 86
Evans, Geraint 56
Evans, Lord 57
Evelyn, John 11, 79

Farthingdown Common 68
Favale, Signor Pasquale 72
Field Studies Council 67
Finsbury Circus 29, 69, *70*, 88, 89
First World War 15
Fishmongers' Hall 8
Fitz-Ailwyn, Henry 8, 20
Fleet River 11, 29, 72, 76
Fleet Street 29, 55, 57, 72, 86, 88, 89
Flower, Charles 51
food imports 41
foreign banks 33
Forest Gate 67
Franklin, Benjamin 84
freedom of the City 13, 14, 16, 27
Frobisher Crescent 51
Fulton, Missouri 79
futures markets 34

Galway, James 56
Garlick Hill 73
Gascoyne, Sir Crisp 20
Geoffrey the Portreeve 7
George I 73
George III 15, 21
George V, Silver Jubilee 9
Gibbons, Orlando 55
Goldsmiths' Hall 71
Gravesend 41
Great Fire 8, 9, *11*, 15, 22, 30, 79, 84, 86
Great Plague 9
Gresham Street 88
Greyfriars Monastery 77
Grey, Lady Jane 14
Grimes, Professor W.F. 62, 86
Guildhall 12–15, *12, 15, 26*, 77, *84*
 crypt *13*

Great Hall 12, 13, 19
 Library 58–60, 58
 magistrates' courts 47
 paving 21
 standard measures *14*
Guildhall School of Music and Drama 24, 48–52, 55–6, *55*
guilds 8

Hall, Sir Peter 51
Harris, Harry 36
Hartnell, Norman 61
Hart Street 72
Headmasters' Conference 57
health 40
Heathrow Airport 41
Henley 73
Henry I 8, 83
Henry III 67
Henry IV 21
Henry V 37
Henry VIII 67, 72
Hess, Myra 56
High Court judges 46
Highgate Wood 68
Hilbery, Mr Justice 47
Hobley, Brian 64
Holborn 73
Honey Lane Market 57
Honourable Artillery Company 17
Hudson, Henry 86
Huggins Hill 64

Inner Temple 88
insurance 31–2
invisible exports 31
Isle of Sheppey 41
Ivan the Terrible 9

Jaffa, Max 56
jobbers 33
John Carpenter Street 55, 56
John, King 8–9
 charter of 8–9
Johnson, Dr 21
Jones, Sir Horace 38, 42, 55, 58
Joyce, William 46
judges 46
judges of the Queen's Bench Division 17
Junior Guildhall 56
Justice Room, Mansion House 47

Kenley Common 68
Kennett, Brackley 22
King Edward IV School 72
Knights Templar 88
Knollys, Constance 73
Knollys, Sir Robert 73

Lake Havasu City 38
Leach, Dr Harry 40
Leadenhall Market 24, 42, *43*
Leadenhall Street 63, 72
Leaver, Sir Christopher 19
Lee, Sir Sidney 57
leisure 89
libraries 58–60
Libraries, Art Galleries and Records Committee 60
Liverpool Street Station 30
livery companies 8, 11, 13, 16, 19
 Accountants 11
 Actuaries 11
 Air Pilots and Navigators 11
 Butchers 76, 84
 Clockmakers 59
 Clothworkers 8, 71, 73

91

Drapers 8
Environmental Cleaners 11
Fishmongers 8
Glaziers 88
Goldsmiths 8, 71
Grocers 8, 88
Haberdashers 8
Ironmongers 8
Mercers 8, 86
Merchant Taylors 8, 11
Musicians 55
Saddlers 86
Salters 8
Skinners 8
Vintners 8, 73, 86
  procession 73, 75
Lloyds Bank 33
Lloyd's of London 25, 31–2, *32*
Local Plan 28–30
Lombard merchants 8
Lombard Street 8
Londinium *6*, 6
London Bridge 25, 35–8, *36*, *37*, *38*, 64, *78*
London Commodity Exchange 34
London International Financial Futures Exchange (title page verso), 34
London Marathon Sports Library 60
London Metal Exchange 34
London Port Health Authority 24, 41
London Symphony Orchestra 50–1, *50*, 56
London Wall 29, 61
Lord Chancellor 16, 46, 47
Lord Chief Justice 17, 46
Lord Mayor of London 7, 8, 9, *9*, 14, 15, 16–22, *17*, *22*, 24, 67, 73
  and judges 46, 47
  coach 17, *18*, 61
  election 16
  household officers 20
  residence 20
Lord Mayor's Banquet 13, 14, *19*, 45, 76
Lord Mayor's Show 17–19, *17*, *18*, *19*, 24, 28, 45, 71, 76
Lundunberg 7
Luxon, Benjamin 56

Mace 9, 20, 24
Magistrates' Courts 47
Magna Carta 9, 60
Mansion House *17*, 20, *21*, 22, 24, 47, 73, 77, 88
Master of the Mint 71
Mazarin, Cardinal 24
McCulloch Oil Corporation 38
Mead, William 46
Mellitus 7
merchant banks 33
merchants 9
Metropolitan Police 45, 46
Middle Temple *28*, 88
Midland Bank 33
Milk Street 8
Mincing Lane 8
Missal of St Botolph 59
Mithras 7, *7*
  Temple of 63, *63*
Monument, the *6*, 35, *35*, 69
Moore, Dudley 56
Moore, Henry 88
More, Sir Thomas 37, 60
mounted police *46*
Mountford, E.W. 46
Museum of London 61–5, *61*, *62*, *65*, 89
music 54–6
Music Committee 56
mynchens 8

Napoleon's invasion 14
National Westminster Bank *25*, 33
Nelson, Admiral Lord 14, 20, 82

Nemon, Oscar 14
Newgate Prison 21, 46
Noise Abatement Act 54
Norfolk, Duke of 13
Normans 8
North West Passage 86
Nunn, Trevor 51

Old Bailey 46–7, *47*
Old Broad Street 88
Old Jewry 46
Old Library, Guildhall 19
open spaces 67–70
Oundle 8

Pankhurst, Emmeline 47
Paternoster Square 89
Paterson, William 11
Paul's Cross *10*
Peelers 45
Penn, William 46
Pepys, Samuel 11, 14, 22, 55, 72, 73, 80, 88
Peter of Colechurch 36, 37
Petrus of Riga 58
Petticoat Lane 44
Philip, Prince 86
Pilgrim Fathers 88
Pitt-Rivers, General 62
Pitt the Younger 15
Pitt, William, Earl of Chatham 14, 15
Plautius, Aulus 6
Pocohontas 86
Police, City of London 45–6
Police, Metropolitan 45, 46
police stations 46
Postman's Park 70
Port and City of London Health Committee 41
Port of London 40–1, *40*
portreeve 7, 8
Poultry 8
Poultry Market, Smithfield 42
Pré, Jacqueline du 56
Previn, André 51
Pudding Lane *6*, 63
Purcell, Henry 55
Putney 36

Queen Elizabeth's Hunting Lodge 67
Queenhithe 64
Queen's Hall 51
Queen's Park, Kilburn 68
Queen's Remembrancer 71, 75
Quit Rents ceremony 75, *77*

Rahere 83, 84
Recorder 28, 46
Records Office, Guildhall 7, *59*, 60
Reed, Talbot Baines 60
Registrar General 40
Remembrancer 26, 28
Rennie, John 36, 37
retail markets 42–4
Richard II 20
Richter, Dr Hans 51
Riddlesdown Common 68
River Fleet 11, 29
River Medway 41
River Roach 41
River Thames *6*, 18, 35, 41
Roman empire 7
Roman Gallery, Museum of London *65*
Roman London 6–7, 63–5, 88
Roman wall 6, 7, *48*, 63
Rome 7, 63, 82
royal charters 7, 8, 9
Royal Courts of Justice 17, 75
Royal Exchange 89
Royal Fusiliers 15
Royal Mint 71
Royal Shakespeare Company 50, 51, 56

Royal Victoria Dock 65
Runnymede 9

St Andrew Undershaft 72, *73*
St Anne and St Agnes 88
St Bartholomew's Hospital 21, 84
St Bartholomew-the-Great 72, *72*, 83
St Benet's, Paul's Wharf *86*, 88
St Botolph's, Aldersgate *70*
St Botolph's, Aldgate 71
St Bride Printing Library 60
St Bride's, Fleet Street 72, 83, 86
St Bridget of Kildare 86
St Dunstan in the East 69
St Ethelburga-the-Virgin 86
St Giles without Cripplegate *48*, 52, 57
St James's, Garlickhythe 73, *83*
St Lawrence Jewry 16, 71, 80, *84*
St Magnus the Martyr 88
St Mary Aldermanbury 79
St Mary at Hill *86*
St Mary Colechurch 36
St Mary-le-Bow 84, *84*
St Michael Paternoster Royal 83
St Olave's, Hart Street 72
St Paul, church of 63
St Paul's Cathedral 5, 35, *26*, 80–3, *80*, 89
  Choir School 83
St Paul's Girls' School 8
St Paul's School 8
St Sepulchre's, Holborn 73
St Stephen Walbrook 88
St Thomas à Becket 36
St Vedast-alias-Foster *82*
Samaritans 88
Sandys, Mr Duncan 48
Saunders, Sir William Sedgewick 67
Saxon invaders 7
Saxon London 7, 63
schools 67
Scott, Sir Giles Gilbert 15
Secondary and Under-Sheriff and High Baliff of Southwark Prothonotary 25, 46, *47*
Second World War 12, 15, 46, 47, 69, 70, 83
Seething Lane 73
Serjeant-at-Arms, Common Cryer and 20, 24, 46
Shakespeare 51, 59
Shakespeare Tower 52
Shaw, James 14
Sheerness 41
shellfish harvest 41
Sheriffs 14, 16, 18, 24, 46, 47, 73
Shoe Lane library 60
Silent Change ceremony 16, *17*, 76
Skellern, Peter 56
Smith, Captain John 86
Smithfield Market 24, 41, 42, *42*, 76, 84
Snow Hill 46
Somerset, Duke of 58
South African War 15
Southwark Bridge 36, *37*
Spitalfields Market 44, 71
Spital Sermon 71
Spring Park 68
Square Mile 35, 41, 89
  churches 79
State Sword 20, 24
Steiner, John 83
Sterndale-Bennett, William 55
Stock Exchange 33, 34, 69
Stow, John 58, 72, 73
Strand 75
Stratford-upon-Avon 51
Sullivan, Sir Arthur 82
Superintendent of Parks and Gardens 70
Surrey, Earl of 13
Sutcliffe, Peter 46

Swan Theatre 51
Swan Upping 73, 75
Swordbearer 20, 24, 46
Synagogue, Bevis Marks 88

Tacitus 6
Tallis, Thomas 55
Teddington Lock 41
Temple Bar 9, 18, *19*
Temple Church 88
Territorial Army 17
Thorndike, Sybil 56
Thorp, John Thomas *22*
Tilbury 35
Tower Bridge 25, 36, 38, *38*
Tower Hamlets, London Borough of 43–4
Tower Hill 14, 89
Tower of London 7, 21, 22, 25, 35, *40*
Tower Pier 35
Trade Exhibition Halls, Barbican Centre 51
traditions 71–7
Trafalgar 14
Trecothick, Barlow 22
Trial of the Pyx ceremony 71
trials, Guildhall 13–14
  Central Criminal Court 46–7
Tudor, Mary 14
Turk, John 73

Upper Thames Street 73, 88

Vanbrugh, Sir John 88
Varah, Revd Chad 88
Vaughan, Chief Justice 46
veterinary services 41
Victoria Embankment 55, 57
Victoria, Queen 36

Walbrook 63, *64*, 88
Warden Point 41
Wardmote 24
Ward, William 57, 68
watch house *45*
watchman 54
Watling Court 63
Watson, Sir Brook 22
Weist Hall 55
Wellington, Duke of 15, 82
West Ham 70
Westminster 35
Westminster Abbey 7, 21
Westminster Bridge 35
Westminster Hall 13, 88
Westminster Palace 7
Wheeler, Sir Mortimer 62
Whispering Gallery 82
Whitehall 63
Whitefriars 54
White Tower 7
Whittington, Richard (Dick) 20, *22*, 56, 58
Whittington, Sir William 20
Whittington Room, Guildhall 58
wholesale markets 42–4
Wilkes, Admiral Charles 22
Wilkes, Israel 22
Wilkes, John 21
William I, charter of 7
William IV and Queen Adelaide 37, *38*
William, Bishop 7
William the Conqueror 7
William Pitt Bridge 36
Winslow, Edward 88
Witley 72
Wood, Sir Henry 51
Wood Street 8, 46
Worde, Wynkyn de 86
Wren, Sir Christopher 11, 79, 80, 82, 84, 86, 88

Yevele, William 88

zoos 41